THE VEGAN ELECTRIC
PRESSURE COOKER COOKBOOK

Teriyaki Tempeh and Broccoli

PAGE 42

Pistachio-Apricot Quinoa

PAGE 26

The VEGAN

ELECTRIC PRESSURE COOKER COOKBOOK

SIMPLE **5-Ingredient** RECIPES
FOR YOUR PLANT-BASED LIFESTYLE

Heather Nicholds

Photography by Becky Stayner

ROCKRIDGE
PRESS

To Jill and JL, the vegan pressure-cooking queens
who have inspired so many—including me!

Contents

8 PIECE-OF-CAKE DESSERTS 103

Introduction

As somewhat of a minimalist, I find that few gadgets or appliances get me excited or feel like a necessity. My electric pressure cooker is one of those rare appliances that was a total game changer—in so many ways. It made healthy cooking easier and quicker, batch-cooking a breeze, and trying new foods much more fun because they took less time to cook.

I knew about stovetop pressure cookers but was intimidated by their use. Figuring out how to get to and maintain the proper pressure and keeping track of cooking time seemed too challenging. Despite guidance from wonderful cooking instructors, such as Jill Nussinow, I just didn't feel sufficiently confident to jump on the pressure cooker bandwagon.

The moment I did was when my dear friend and pressure-cooking enthusiast JL Fields explained how electric pressure cookers work: You set the pressure and time and walk away while it does the work! You could practically see the lightbulb go on over my head during our live video chat.

My inner dialogue went something like this: "Wait—I can put the beans in, set the time, let them do their thing, and just come back to purée them into hummus? Where do I get one of these magical devices?"

I had stopped cooking dried beans because the cost of energy where I lived was so high that buying canned beans was cheaper. Although I felt horrible about putting so many aluminum cans in the recycling bin each week, I felt even worse about three hours of electricity use and cost.

So, when I got my electric pressure cooker, it was like the dawn of a new era. It lifted a huge weight off my environmentalist soul to be able to cook dried beans without using a huge amount of precious Earth resources.

At first, all I did was make big batches of plain beans and whole grains, which I would add to other dishes throughout the week. It was a great way to start, but I branched out when I realized I could make soups and whole meals in record time.

My goal with this book is to help you make fast, delicious vegan meals that maximize nutrition using your electric pressure cooker. All the recipes in this book have five things in common:

> They can be cooked entirely in your electric pressure cooker.

> They are vegan.

> They are easy to make.

> They use fresh, wholesome ingredients.

> They require only five core ingredients.

Oh, and one other thing: These recipes all taste good; otherwise, we wouldn't eat them! Because everyone's taste buds are different, I usually give a basic recipe and then suggest optional seasonings to boost flavor, along with notes to guide you.

So, dig in. This cookbook is perfect for anyone who is pressed for time and searching for healthy, economical, and tasty plant-based meals.

CHAPTER 1

The Basics of Electric Pressure Cooking

Before we jump into the recipes, let's review how an electric pressure cooker works and how to cook with it. Here's what you'll find in this chapter:

> information on the various kinds of electric pressure cookers available

> descriptions of the easy-to-use functions that make an electric pressure cooker the most essential item in your vegan kitchen

> the basics of how to cook plant foods in your electric pressure cooker

> guidelines on kitchen safety

> tips on how to clean and care for your electric pressure cooker

> answers to the most common questions about vegan electric pressure cooking

Selecting Your New Electric Pressure Cooker

You'll find many options when you start shopping for an electric pressure cooker. Right now, the most popular model—and thus one for which accessories and replacement parts are easiest to find—is the Instant Pot®. But there are lots of others pressure cooker and multi-cooker choices. Here's a brief comparison of four top brands:

	Instant Pot® Duo	Fagor Lux Multi-Cooker	Cuisinart Electric Pressure Cooker	Breville Fast Slow Pro™
Sizes	3, 6, 8 quarts	4, 6, 8 quarts	4, 6, 8 quarts	6 quarts
Cooking Settings	Pressure Cook (high and low), Slow Cook, Sauté/Simmer, Steam, Soup, Meat/Stew, Bean/Chili, Poultry, Rice, Multigrain, Porridge, Yogurt, Manual, Keep Warm	Pressure Cook (high and low), Slow Cook (high and low), Simmer, Sauté, Steam, Brown, Yogurt, White Rice, Brown Rice, Risotto, Keep Warm	Pressure Cook (high and low), Sauté, Brown, Simmer, Keep Warm	Pressure Cook (11 settings), Slow Cook (high and low), Steam, Sear, Sauté, Reduce, Keep Warm
Pressure Release Settings	Quick or Natural	Quick or Natural	Quick or Natural	Quick, Pulse, or Natural
Special Features	Stainless steel pot, delay start	Stainless steel pot, delay start, adjustable temperature and timer		Altitude-adjust function, custom pressure cook setting
Best Feature	Variety of functions with automated temperature control	Variety of functions with precise temperature control	Simple to use and get started	Precise settings (rather than preprogrammed)

As for which size to get, here's a general guideline: A 3- or 4-quart model makes enough food for one or two people, a 6-quart model makes enough for three or four people, and an 8-quart model makes enough for four or five people. But keep in mind that although you may be cooking for only one or two people at each meal, it's often handy to batch-cook grains, beans, soups, and sauces so you can have enough for a week's worth of meals—or to stock your freezer.

Understanding Your Electric Pressure Cooker

Pressure cookers work by increasing the boiling point of water. When you put a regular pot on the stove, the liquid inside will heat up until it hits the boiling point (212°F for water) and stay at that temperature. Any extra heat will just cause the water to turn into steam, which dissipates. The food inside the pot cooks at a rate limited by the boiling point (temperature) of the water. The boiling point of water is a constant—but one that changes depending on the surrounding pressure.

A pressure cooker has a sealed container, so the steam that's created doesn't escape. The steam expands until it reaches the maximum volume of the pressure cooker's container, and then it starts to compress, which increases the pressure. As the pressure increases, the temperature of the steam and the liquid also increases—above the normal boiling point. The water and steam inside a pressure cooker can reach a temperature of 250°F. It's that higher temperature that makes the food inside cook faster than in a regular pot on the stove. It's also why pressure cooker recipes always need to include liquid.

As you can imagine, if we're going to create that kind of pressure in our kitchen, we need to feel confident the pot will contain it. The old-fashioned type of stovetop pressure cookers could explode due to poor-quality materials and a lack of safety features. On top of that worry, you had to keep track of the cooking time so you'd know when to start releasing the pressure.

Modern pressure cookers have improved drastically from earlier models. They have valves that vent excess steam to maintain the right pressure, backup safety valves, and better locking mechanisms to keep the lid secure. Furthermore, electric pressure cookers maintain the temperature and shut off automatically based on the setting and time you input.

Here are the three basic types of pressure cookers, listed in order from least to most safe and efficient:

› Weighted valve (jiggle-top) pressure cooker: This pressure cooker is the one your grandmother probably had. It's heated on the stove, and the valve sits on top of a vent where it is lifted by the steam. Once it reaches a sufficiently high pressure, it makes a hissing noise as it lifts the valve slightly, and it will start to rock from side to side. Maintaining the right pressure involves keeping the heat at the right temperature to keep the valve rocking. You keep track of the time at pressure when it starts to hiss and rock and turn off the heat to start releasing the pressure.

› Spring-loaded valve pressure cooker: This cooker features the newer generation of valve, which is designed to keep the vent open until the pressure builds, pushing the valve up and closing it. If the pressure gets too high, the valve is pushed up further, which opens it to let steam escape and return to the correct pressure. The valve is integrated with the locking mechanism of the lid, so you can't open the lid until the pressure comes down. On stovetop models, you need to maintain the correct temperature and keep track of the time at pressure.

› Electric pressure cooker: This cooker uses a spring-loaded valve but has an electric cooking base, so you can set the pressure you want, and the cooker will automatically maintain the correct temperature. It also has a timer, so you can set the time you want at pressure, and it will count down once it gets to pressure.

There are lots of accessories to help you maximize your electric pressure cooker's functionality. Here are some that might come in handy:

› Most pressure cookers come with a nonstick inner pot, which can get scratched. For your model, you might be able to buy a stainless steel inner pot, which won't scratch and thus may last a lot longer.

› If you don't have a stainless steel inner pot, you'll want to have a variety of silicone-tipped utensils to help ensure that the nonstick coating doesn't get scratched.

› Your electric pressure cooker will probably come with a trivet, which allows you to elevate a steamer basket from the bottom of the pot.

› Steamer baskets are sold in pressure cooker accessory packs, but you can use any regular steaming basket that fits inside the pot. The folding leaf–style version works well, or you can use a traditional bamboo steamer.

› Ramekins and other heat-proof dishes that fit inside the inner pot come in handy for vegetable dishes that you don't want to get too watery, as well as for pies and crumbles.

› Accessory packs often come with a springform pan, which is great for making pies because you can remove the outer ring for slicing.

› Silicone "pinch" mitts are useful for picking up pans and steaming baskets because they have more grip than regular oven mitts.

› Silicone "helper handles" allow you to safely and easily pick up a pie or other dish that fills the inside of your pressure cooker pot. You can also make your own by folding a long piece of aluminum foil in thirds and placing it in the pot, with the ends coming up and over the top. Simply place the dish on top of the foil "sling," and tuck in the ends so you can lock and seal the lid properly.

LOCKING THE LID AND RELEASING PRESSURE

Any time you use the pressure-cooking functions, you need to ensure that the lid is locked and the valve is set to seal. If you're using functions that do not involve cooking under pressure, such as Sauté, Brown, Slow Cook, Simmer, or Keep Warm, you can simply place the lid on top—there's no need to lock it in place.

Once the pressure builds and the cooking is complete, it's time to release that pressure with either the natural or the quick release method. The biggest difference between the two release methods is that pressure and heat are maintained in the pot longer with a natural release, so the food will continue to cook a bit. Additionally, the quick release lets out the steam rather than condensing it back into the dish.

A natural release is perfect for beans and grains; a little extra cook time and moisture help soften them. A quick release is preferable for vegetables, which we don't want to get too soft.

If you want a bit more cook time but also want to let off some of the steam, you can allow the pressure to decrease naturally for a certain amount of time and then quickly release the remaining pressure.

Pressure Cooking and High Altitude

Air pressure drops at higher altitudes, which means that the boiling point of water also drops. So, for any given pressure setting, food will take longer to cook. If your kitchen is more than 2,000 feet above sea level, you will need to increase the cooking times in this book by about 5 percent for every 1,000 feet above that altitude.

Say you're cooking brown rice and the recipe tells you to set the cook time for 10 minutes under high pressure. If you're cooking in New York City, which is at sea level, you simply set your electric pressure cooker for 10 minutes. But if you're cooking in Salt Lake City, which is about 4,000 feet above sea level, you need to increase your cooking time by 10 percent, which will bring you to 11 minutes. If you're cooking in Cusco, Peru, which is about 11,000 feet above sea level, you need to increase your cooking time by 45 percent, so you'll need to set the timer for 15 minutes.

Common Misconceptions about Cooking with Electric Pressure Cookers

It's too expensive! Brown rice and dried lentils are some of the cheapest vegan food items in the grocery store, and they give you more protein and nutrients per dollar than animal foods.

It's too difficult to figure out! At its most basic level, pressure cooking involves putting food and water in a pot and setting the time. This is actually the easiest way to cook!

Everything will come out mushy! You'll soon find that pressure cooking helps foods such as brown rice maintain more of their texture than regular stovetop cooking. If you cook foods at the recommended pressure and time setting, they should come out perfectly cooked. You can also use a steaming basket to prevent vegetables from getting mushy.

I don't want another appliance! The electric pressure cooker takes the place of a rice cooker and a slow cooker—and it saves you time.

Pressure cooking destroys all the nutrients! Because foods cook quickly under pressure, they retain more nutrients than they do when they are prepared using other techniques, such as boiling, steaming, baking, or roasting. And if you cook your vegetables in a steaming basket above the water, they'll retain even more nutrients.

ELECTRIC PRESSURE COOKER UNIVERSAL SETTINGS

You'll be using the easy settings on your electric pressure cooker to cook all the recipes in this book. These settings are perfect for vegan cooking on busy weeknights and jam-packed weekends, or batch-cooking for meal prep. The beauty of the electric pressure cooker is that you can set it and forget it, as with a rice cooker or slow cooker, while also reducing the cooking time. With additional features such as Sauté and Simmer, you can use multiple cooking methods for a meal right in one pot, which cuts down on the amount of dishwashing you need to do as well.

If you want to make sure your machine works before trying specific recipes, do a test run with just water. Put 3 or 4 cups of water into the pot, close and lock the lid, and then set the cooker to High Pressure for 5 minutes. You should hear some steam release after a few minutes, and then the cooker should seal and start to count down the time. When the timer beeps, let the pressure release naturally (or try a quick release—see your user manual for instructions). When you hear the lid unlock, you can safely open the pot. You should find that not much of the water has evaporated.

Here's a quick run-down of the various settings called for in this cookbook:

High Pressure This setting increases the pressure inside the pot to increase the boiling temperature of water to between 240°F and 250°F, which decreases the time that foods need to cook. High Pressure is the setting most often used in pressure cooker recipes for foods such as beans, grains, root vegetables, and pastas.

Low Pressure This setting increases the pressure inside the pot to increase the boiling temperature of water to between 220°F and 230°F. Foods cook faster than on the stovetop, but not as fast as at high pressure. This setting can be useful for cooking more delicate vegetables, such as green beans or asparagus.

Slow Cook/Simmer This setting adjusts the heat to the equivalent of low on a stovetop and lets you slow cook a dish. You can also continue cooking something if the time at pressure wasn't quite enough, or if you need to reduce some of the liquid after pressure cooking to finish a dish.

Sauté This setting adjusts the heat to the equivalent of medium-high on a stovetop so that you can soften vegetables, toast rice for pilaf, or reduce a sauce. Use some oil, water, or broth for cooking garlic, ginger, onion, and other vegetables on this setting.

Brown This setting adjusts the heat to the equivalent of high on a stovetop so you can sear vegetables. If you brown food before pressure cooking, it takes less time to get up to pressure, as the contents are already hot. Use some oil, water, or broth for cooking garlic, ginger, onion, and other vegetables on this setting, and leave the lid off.

Programmed Settings The Instant Pot® and some other multi-cookers also have several programmed functions that allow you to press a single button, rather than setting the pressure and time yourself. For example, if you press the Rice button, it will set the time and pressure for cooking white rice, which should be High Pressure for 3 to 4 minutes. The Multigrain button is for brown rice, which starts with 50 minutes on Simmer, then switches to High Pressure for 9 minutes.

Kitchen Safety Guide

1. Each time you use your electric pressure cooker, before you start cooking, check that the lid's rubber seal is in good shape and the vent is clean and clear, with no stuck-on food or foam.

2. Always use some liquid in the pot. If you want to cook a vegetable without submerging it, use a pan or a steaming basket elevated on a trivet, but make sure to have some liquid in the bottom of the pot.

3. Never fill the pot higher than the maximum fill line. In addition, limit the contents of the pot to half full for foods that expand or foam a bit (such as rice and pasta) and to no more than one-third full for beans and lentils, as they expand and foam even more. Adding a bit of oil to the pot with grains, beans, and pasta can help minimize foaming.

4. Always check that the valve is set to Seal before you set the cook time. If it's set to Release Pressure, food won't cook properly, and you may burn your fingers if you try to rotate the valve back to Seal while the heat is on.

5. To safely do a quick release, make sure your hands and face are not above where the steam will release. You can use a kitchen utensil to push the valve to release the steam if you want to be sure. Simply push to rotate the valve to Release, and let the steam vent until the lid unlocks. Never force the lid open—it will click to unlock when the pressure is low enough that you can safely open it.

6. When lifting the lid after cooking, tilt it away from you to avoid getting hot steam in your face or having anything spatter up toward you. This is especially important if you do a quick pressure release.

7. Read and follow your electric pressure cooker model's user manual. Your model may differ in certain ways from these general guidelines, and you should always defer to the manufacturer's instructions. Your manual will also list cooking times for various foods, and these may be more accurate than the general times listed here.

Cooking Basics for Plant Foods

The electric pressure cooker does an excellent job of cooking plant foods such as beans, grains, and starchy vegetables—and much more quickly than on the stovetop. Here are some tips to make starting out with your pressure cooker as easy as possible:

Beans (black, white, kidney, pinto, black-eyed peas, chickpeas, etc.) and legumes (all kinds of lentils) All you need to do is put them in the pot with plenty of water—cover them by at least 1 inch—and set the time on high pressure according to the bean. Lentils cook fairly quickly, while larger beans and chickpeas take a bit longer. Check your pressure cooker's manual for exact times. If you soak the beans in advance, they will take even less time to cook.

Starchy vegetables (potatoes, sweet potatoes, squash, beets, carrots, etc.) These vegetables won't absorb water while they cook, so you need to add only enough water to keep the bottom of the pot from drying out. Cut-up vegetables take less time to cook than whole vegetables. You can also put your vegetables in a steaming basket above the water to retain more of their nutrients and keep them from getting too watery; using a steamer also allows you to cook something else below at the same time.

Whole grains (brown rice, steel-cut oats, barley, millet, quinoa, and so on) Because there isn't any water evaporation in the pressure cooker, you can use less water than you would on a stovetop. The general rule of thumb for stovetop cooking is 2 cups of water for each 1 cup of grain, but in the pressure cooker you can generally use 1¼ cups of water for each 1 cup of grain. Select High Pressure, and refer to your pressure cooker's manual for exact times for each grain. I prefer to do a natural release with whole grains, so I set the timer for a minute or two less than typically called for and use a bit less electricity as they continue cooking while the pressure releases.

THE BEST AND WORST FOODS FOR VEGAN PRESSURE COOKING

Some foods are especially great to cook in your electric pressure cooker—and some are not.

Best

1. Beans and lentils cook perfectly and in much less time than on the stovetop, making it feasible in daily life—and with rising electricity costs—to cook them from dried rather than buying canned.

2. Whole grains, such as rice and quinoa, also cook perfectly and in less time than on the stovetop.

3. Potatoes and sweet potatoes can be cooked whole or chopped, on their own or in a dish.

4. Beets can also be cooked whole or chopped. This vegetable really benefits nutritionally from shorter cooking times, as the longer it cooks, the more its unique phytonutrients are broken down.

5. Winter squash can be cooked whole in your pressure cooker, meaning you don't have to wrestle with peeling and seeding a raw squash.

Worst

1. Greens and fresh herbs don't need much cooking, so they get way too soft in the pressure cooker. Add them to the pot after the pressure is released, and let them wilt in the residual heat. If you like your greens cooked a little more, turn the pressure cooker to Sauté or Simmer and cook for a few minutes with the lid off to finish.

2. Green beans and asparagus can definitely be cooked in a pressure cooker, but you need to be very careful about how long they cook, as they can become overly soft and you have no way to know if this is happening.

3. Rolled oats cook quickly on their own and don't really benefit from the pressure cooker. They also become too thick.

4. Thick sauces will just bubble and spurt in your pressure cooker. Without steam, the valve won't register that the pot has come up to pressure, and the unit will shut itself off.

5. Hard alcohol (anything with a higher alcohol percentage than wine or beer) can ignite when the pressure releases. Avoid putting anything like rum or vodka in a dish when it's under pressure.

When learning to pressure cook, you can easily avoid some common mistakes. Here are some hacks to get you on top of the vegan pressure cooking game from the start:

› When cooking rice or beans, make sure you have enough liquid for them to cook properly, because they absorb liquid as they cook. If in doubt, refer to your electric pressure cooker model's user manual for correct quantities.

› Beans take a lot longer to cook than other foods, so you can't usually cook them with anything else. Cook beans on their own first, in a big batch, and then add them to dishes through the week.

› Vegetables release liquid when they cook, so cooking them with water can leave them mushy and bland. Unless you're making soup or cooking whole vegetables, the best strategy for cooking vegetables is to use a steamer basket or dish elevated above the water.

› If you're trying a new food in the pressure cooker and you're not sure how long to cook it, err on the low side of the time setting. You can always use the Sauté or Simmer function to finish it once the pressure releases.

› Regular recipes and slow cooker recipes can come out beautifully in a pressure cooker if they are based on a liquid cooking method—but you have to modify the time. A general rule of thumb is to divide a regular recipe's cooking time in half or use 10 percent of a slow cooker recipe's cooking time. Also, as there's barely any evaporation, you may need to reduce the liquid content slightly to make sure the flavor isn't diluted.

Essential Ingredients
to Keep Stocked

FRIDGE AND FREEZER

> Frozen vegetables (corn, kale, peas, spinach) are great to have on hand—add them to any dish to bump up the vegetable content. You'll usually want to toss them in after pressure cooking because they're already cooked and just need to thaw.

> Fruit provides natural sweetness and plenty of vitamins, minerals, and antioxidants to keep us healthy and happy.

> Garlic and ginger are the base for many great soups and sauces. You can use garlic powder or ground ginger, but the fresh versions provide the most nutrients and antioxidants.

> Onions and leeks contribute a savory flavor to vegetable dishes to keep them from tasting like baby food.

> Starchy vegetables (beets, potatoes, squash) are perfect for pressure cooking. You'll find lots of recipes in this book that include them.

PANTRY

> Beans (black, chickpeas, kidney, white) can be batch-cooked during the weekend so you have them throughout the week for adding to salads and soups or making healthy, protein-packed dips.

> Oil creates a depth of texture and flavor when used in cooking. Olive, coconut, and toasted sesame are the main oils used in this book.

> Spices and herbs bring flavor to foods. Most of what we love about our favorite dishes are the spices and herbs used to season them. Powdered garlic and onion are sometimes better than fresh in a pressure cooker dish, since their flavors get diluted.

> Vinegars brighten sauces and add tangy flavor to foods. Balsamic, apple cider, rice, and wine vinegars are used throughout the book.

> Whole grains (barley, quinoa, rice, steel-cut oats) can be used in specific dishes, or they can be cooked in big batches to accompany meals throughout the week.

Cleaning and Caring for Your Electric Pressure Cooker

Caring for your electric pressure cooker is pretty simple. Most standard pots have a nonstick coating that can be easily scratched by metal utensils or harsh scrubbing pads, so it's best to transfer the food to a serving or storage container and then wash the pot right away. If anything is stuck on the bottom, soak the pot in warm, soapy water and come back to it later.

To clean the lid, pull out the inner piece and remove the silicone ring so you can fully clean every part. You can even remove the valve from the lid to clean it, then push a pipe cleaner through it to release any food or foam that is stuck inside.

Never put the cooking base or electric cord in water. Use a damp cloth or sponge to gently wipe the outside of your unit and the cord if they get dirty. You also need to clean around the top, under the lip in which the pot sits, as bits of food will fall in there every so often. If you need to wipe the heating element itself, unplug the unit and use a dry cloth.

Frequently Asked Questions

Can a pressure cooker explode?
Although electric pressure cookers are much safer than older stovetop models, you do need to follow basic safety guidelines to make sure there are no mishaps. The main safety rules are outlined in the previous section (see page 10), like making sure you use enough liquid and don't overfill the pot. Always read and follow the specific guidelines in your model's user manual.

Do these vegan recipes provide enough protein?
Overall, a vegan diet can give us all the protein we need. The individual recipes in this book are not necessarily fully balanced on their own; they are designed to be mixed and matched to create balanced and nutrient-dense vegan meals. Some recipes offer suggestions for what to pair them with for flavor and nutrition.

What do you mean by "five ingredients"?

Each recipe calls for five core ingredients. Items you normally keep on hand, such as salt, water, oil, vinegar, and dried spices and herbs are not counted as core ingredients; any exotic or obscure ingredients are usually listed as optional.

How much time can I save?

Electric pressure cooking generally takes about half the time of regular stovetop cooking (or even less than that in the case of beans). However, because it takes time to get up to pressure and then to release it, the total time often winds up about the same. What you're really saving on is the active time of watching and waiting while the water comes to a boil and then turning down the heat, and also the electricity or gas cost of that time.

Veggie Fried Rice

PAGE 24

CHAPTER 2

Get Going with Grains

With an electric pressure cooker, you get all the set-it-and-forget-it benefits of a rice cooker, but you can shave off a huge amount of cooking time, which is particularly handy for grains that take a long time to cook. Plus, you don't have to monitor your rice as it comes to a boil, then manage the heat setting to make sure it doesn't boil over and create a sticky mess on your stovetop.

Whole grains provide a multitude of nutrients to our bodies and have been a primary source of energy for humans for millennia. Reducing cooking time and effort with your pressure cooker means you can explore more of the ancient grains, such as freekeh, millet, and quinoa, each of which has a unique nutritional profile and assortment of phytonutrient properties to contribute to your diet.

Easy on Your Wallet

Buying whole grains in bulk is a great way to save money and reduce plastic waste. Grains can be stored for up to 6 months if they are sealed properly and kept in a cool, dry place. You can also keep them in the freezer for up to one year. Glass mason jars or clean pasta sauce jars are a great way to store whole grains and dried beans so you can see at a glance exactly what you have on hand.

Cilantro-Lime Brown and Wild Rice

Infuse wholesome brown rice with zesty lime, and pair it with fresh cilantro to make a base for a bowl with Taco/Burrito Filling (page 34) or Chipotle Chickpeas (page 37) and some cherry tomatoes and corn. This rice mix is also lovely tossed with mango chunks and shelled edamame. *Serves 4*

BUDGET-FRIENDLY, GLUTEN-FREE, NUT-FREE, SOY-FREE

Prep time: 5 minutes · Cooking setting: High Pressure, 10 minutes · Release: Natural · Total time: 30 minutes

★ 1 cup brown or white rice

★ ¼ cup wild rice, or more brown or white rice

★ Grated zest and juice of 1 lime

1½ cups water

Pinch salt, plus more as needed

★ ¼ cup fresh cilantro, chopped

1 tablespoon coconut oil (optional)

1. In your electric pressure cooker's cooking pot, combine the brown rice, wild rice, lime zest and juice, water, and salt. Close and lock the lid and ensure the pressure valve is sealed, then select High Pressure and set the time for 10 minutes (or 3 minutes if using white rice).

2. When the cook time is complete, let the pressure release naturally, about 15 minutes.

3. Once all the pressure has released, carefully unlock and remove the lid. Gently stir in the cilantro and coconut oil (if using). Taste and season with more salt, if needed.

Ingredient tip: Use a fine grater, Microplane, or zester to take off the very outer layer from your lime. The zest is bursting with flavor and antioxidants! If you love lime, like me, you may want to add the zest and juice of a second lime!

PER SERVING Calories: 241; Total fat: 5g; Protein: 5g; Sodium: 5mg; Fiber: 3g

Creamy Squash Risotto

You can make a healthy brown rice risotto so much faster using the pressure cooker than on the stovetop, with squash added for extra nutrients and creaminess. Use acorn, buttercup, butternut, kabocha, or whatever winter squash you like best.
Serves 4

BUDGET-FRIENDLY, GLUTEN-FREE, NUT-FREE, SOY-FREE

Prep time: 10 minutes · Cooking setting: Sauté, 9 minutes, then High Pressure, 10 minutes
Release: Natural · Total time: 45 minutes

★ 1 Vidalia onion, diced

1 teaspoon olive oil or coconut oil

★ 1½ cups short-grain brown rice or white rice

★ 3 cups vegetable broth

½ teaspoon salt

★ ½ large squash or 1 small squash, peeled, seeded, and chopped (about 4 cups)

★ ¼ cup nutritional yeast

1 tablespoon dried sage *or* 1 teaspoon ground sage

1 teaspoon garlic powder (optional)

½ teaspoon ground nutmeg (optional)

Freshly ground black pepper

1. On your electric pressure cooker, select Sauté. Add the onion and oil and cook for 4 to 5 minutes, stirring occasionally, until the onion is browned. Add the rice and toss to coat with the oil. Toast for 3 to 4 minutes, stirring occasionally to prevent burning. Once you smell a toasty aroma from the rice, turn off the cooker.

2. Add the vegetable broth, salt, and squash to the pressure cooker. Close and lock the lid and ensure the pressure valve is sealed, then select High Pressure and set the time for 10 minutes (or 3 minutes if using white rice).

3. When the cook time is complete, let the pressure release naturally, about 15 minutes.

➤

4. Once all the pressure has released, carefully unlock and remove the lid. Add the nutritional yeast, sage, garlic powder (if using), and nutmeg (if using). Using a wooden spoon or spatula, stir to break up the squash and mix it into the rice. Stir with a bit of force, to make sure the rice and squash combine to create a creamy texture. Season with pepper and serve.

Preparation tip: If you'd like more moisture and creaminess, add about ¼ cup unsweetened nondairy milk and/or 1 to 2 tablespoons vegan margarine, select Sauté or Simmer, and cook for a few minutes more at step 4.

PER SERVING Calories: 398; Total fat: 4g; Protein: 13g; Sodium: 306mg; Fiber: 9g

Mushroom and Millet Pilaf

Millet is a super nutritious grain that doesn't get nearly as much attention as quinoa or amaranth. It's naturally gluten-free and a good source of manganese, magnesium, and fiber. Another bonus: It's easily grown in North America, so it requires a lot less shipping than quinoa for those of us who live here. *Serves 4*

BUDGET-FRIENDLY, GLUTEN-FREE, NUT-FREE, SOY-FREE

Prep time: 10 minutes · Cooking setting: Sauté, 10 minutes, then High Pressure, 10 minutes
Release: Natural · Total time: 45 minutes

---

* ★ 4 ounces mushrooms, sliced (about 1½ cups)
* ★ ½ onion, diced
* ★ 1 or 2 garlic cloves, minced
* 1 tablespoon olive oil *or* 2 tablespoons water or vegetable broth
* ★ 1 cup millet
* 2 to 3 teaspoons dried thyme *or* 1 teaspoon ground thyme
* 2 cups water or vegetable broth
* ¼ teaspoon salt

1. On your electric pressure cooker, select Sauté. Add the mushrooms, onion, garlic, and olive oil. Cook for 6 to 7 minutes, stirring occasionally, until the onion is softened and slightly browned. Add the millet and thyme and toss to coat with the oil. Toast for 4 to 5 minutes, stirring occasionally to prevent burning.

2. Add the water and salt. Cancel Sauté.

3. Close and lock the lid and ensure the pressure valve is sealed, then select High Pressure and set the time for 10 minutes.

4. When the cook time is complete, let the pressure release naturally, about 15 minutes.

5. Once all the pressure has released, carefully unlock and remove the lid.

Preparation tip: If you use vegetable broth, you may not need as much thyme.

PER SERVING Calories: 237; Total fat: 6g; Protein: 7g; Sodium: 151mg; Fiber: 5g

Veggie Fried Rice

Use your electric pressure cooker for both cooking the rice and then sautéing ("frying") it with the veggies. You can do this with regular brown rice, or try red rice for a change. This dish goes perfectly with fresh greens and sliced avocado. *Serves 4*

BUDGET-FRIENDLY, GLUTEN-FREE, NUT-FREE

Prep time: 10 minutes · Cooking setting: High Pressure, 10 minutes, then Sauté, 5 minutes
Release: Natural for 10 minutes, then Quick · Total time: 40 minutes

---

★ 1½ cups brown rice or white rice

2 cups water

Pinch salt

★ 2 carrots, scrubbed or peeled and diced

★ 2 scallions, chopped

★ 1 cup peas or shelled edamame

★ ½ (14-ounce) package firm or extra-firm tofu, crumbled (optional)

1 to 2 tablespoons toasted sesame oil

1 tablespoon olive oil (optional)

½ teaspoon ground turmeric (optional)

Salt

Freshly ground black pepper

1. In your electric pressure cooker's cooking pot, combine the rice, water, and salt. Close and lock the lid and ensure the pressure valve is sealed, then select High Pressure and set the time for 10 minutes.

2. When the cook time is complete, let the pressure release naturally for 10 minutes (or 3 minutes if using white rice), then quick release any remaining pressure, being careful not to get your fingers or face near the steam release.

3. Once all the pressure has released, carefully unlock and remove the lid. Push the rice to one side (or scoop it out of the pot) and select Sauté.

4. To the open side of the cooking pot, add the carrots, scallions, peas, tofu (if using), sesame oil, olive oil (if using), and turmeric (if using). Sauté for 3 to 4 minutes, stirring occasionally, until the vegetables are softened. Stir the rice into the veggies. Taste and season with salt and pepper, then cook for another 1 to 2 minutes.

Ingredient tip: Help your tofu absorb more flavor by pressing out some of its moisture before you add it to the rice. Simply place it in a tofu press or between 2 small cutting boards with a book on top for about 10 minutes.

PER SERVING Calories: 436; Total fat: 12g; Protein: 18g; Sodium: 28mg; Fiber: 7g

Cranberry Barley Stuffing

This makes a great side dish to serve with some Cinnamon Chickpeas (page 38) and green beans, and it's also delicious baked inside a winter squash for a holiday meal.
Serves 4

BUDGET-FRIENDLY, GLUTEN-FREE, NUT-FREE, SOY-FREE

Prep time: 10 minutes · Cooking setting: Sauté, 5 minutes, then High Pressure, 20 minutes
Release: Natural · Total time: 50 minutes

★ ½ onion, diced

1 to 2 teaspoons olive oil

★ 1 cup pearl barley, rinsed and drained

★ ½ cup dried cranberries, raisins, or chopped sun-dried tomatoes

1½ cups water or vegetable broth

2 tablespoons dried thyme or sage

½ teaspoon salt, plus more as needed

★ ½ cup fresh parsley, chopped

1. On your electric pressure cooker, select Sauté. Add the onion and olive oil and cook for 4 to 5 minutes, stirring occasionally, until the onion is softened.

2. Stir in the barley, cranberries, water, thyme, and salt. Cancel Sauté.

3. Close and lock the lid and ensure the pressure valve is sealed, then select High Pressure and set the time for 20 minutes.

4. When the cook time is complete, let the pressure release naturally, about 15 minutes.

5. Once all the pressure has released, carefully unlock and remove the lid. Stir in the parsley. Taste and season with more salt, if needed.

Ingredient tip: Barley can get a bit dusty, so it's best to rinse it with water and drain fully before you add it to the pot.

PER SERVING Calories: 287; Total fat: 2g; Protein: 6g; Sodium: 302mg; Fiber: 11g

Pistachio-Apricot Quinoa

This lovely and refreshing mix of flavors and textures is sure to be a hit for weeknight dinners or potluck picnics. It's perfect for summer but can add a splash of sunshine to winter meals as well. *Serves 4*

GLUTEN-FREE, SOY-FREE

Prep time: 10 minutes · Cooking setting: High Pressure, 2 minutes
Release: Natural for 10 minutes, then Quick · Total time: 30 minutes

---

★ 1½ cups quinoa, rinsed and drained

★ ⅓ cup dried apricots, chopped

1¾ cups water

Pinch salt, plus more as needed

★ ¼ red onion, diced, soaked in water, and drained

★ ⅓ cup shelled pistachios, chopped

★ Grated zest and juice of 1 orange

Freshly ground black pepper

Olive oil, for drizzling (optional)

1. In your electric pressure cooker's cooking pot, combine the quinoa, apricots, water, and salt. Close and lock the lid and ensure the pressure valve is sealed, then select High Pressure and set the time for 2 minutes.

2. When the cook time is complete, let the pressure release naturally for 10 minutes, then quick release any remaining pressure, being careful not to get your fingers or face near the steam release.

3. Once all the pressure has released, carefully unlock and remove the lid. While the quinoa is hot, stir in the drained onion, pistachios, and orange zest and juice. Taste and season with salt and pepper, then add a drizzle of olive oil, if you like. Serve warm or chilled.

Preparation tip: Soaking the onion in water helps soften its bite. If you don't like raw red onion, substitute chopped scallions, which have a milder onion flavor.

PER SERVING Calories: 412; Total fat: 13g; Protein: 14g; Sodium: 7mg; Fiber: 9g

Toasted Bulgur Tabbouleh

Toasting the bulgur before cooking it lends a slightly nuttier taste to this tabbouleh—and also helps it come to pressure faster. Bump up the flavor with some chopped fresh mint and chopped cucumber for extra crunch, or toss in some Tofu Feta (page 43). Pair the tabbouleh with a veggie burger or roasted portobello mushroom, or put it in a wrap or a pita with some hummus. *Serves 4*

BUDGET-FRIENDLY, NUT-FREE, SOY-FREE

Prep time: 10 minutes · Cooking setting: Sauté, 8 minutes, then High Pressure, 5 minutes
Release: Natural · Total time: 40 minutes

---

* ✸ 2 lemons
* ✸ 1 cup coarse bulgur wheat
  1½ cups water
  Pinch salt
* ✸ ½ red onion, diced, soaked in water, and drained
* ✸ 1 cup cherry tomatoes, quartered
* ✸ 1 cup fresh parsley, stemmed and chopped
  1 to 2 tablespoons olive oil (optional)
  Freshly ground black pepper

1. Zest and juice 1 lemon and set aside. Cut the other lemon into wedges and set aside.

2. On your electric pressure cooker, select Sauté. Add the bulgur wheat and cook for 7 to 8 minutes, stirring occasionally to avoid burning. Cancel Sauté.

3. Add the water and salt. Close and lock the lid and ensure the pressure valve is sealed, then select High Pressure and set the time for 5 minutes.

4. When the cook time is complete, let the pressure release naturally, about 15 minutes.

5. Once all the pressure has released, carefully unlock and remove the lid. Add the drained onion, tomatoes, parsley, and lemon zest. Gently toss to combine. Drizzle with the lemon juice and olive oil (if using). Season with pepper and serve with lemon wedges for squeezing.

Ingredient tip: You can use full-size tomatoes for this, but you'll want to drain them after chopping to remove excess water, which dilutes the flavor of the salad.

PER SERVING Calories: 174; Total fat: 4g; Protein: 5g; Sodium: 91mg; Fiber: 8g

Freekeh with Toasted Sesame Dressing

Freekeh is a whole grain and a form of wheat. It cooks up to a texture similar to bulgur wheat, so you can substitute freekeh in Toasted Bulgur Tabbouleh (page 27) or anything else you'd use bulgur in. This salad is lovely served with Cinnamon Chickpeas (page 38) and fresh massaged kale, Black-Eyed Peas and Collard Greens (page 39), or a bowl of Golden Carrot and Cauliflower Soup (page 53). *Serves 4 to 6*

BUDGET-FRIENDLY, NUT-FREE, SOY-FREE

Prep time: 5 minutes · Cooking setting: High Pressure, 10 minutes

Release: Natural for 10 minutes, then Quick · Total time: 30 minutes

---

★ 1½ cups freekeh or bulgur wheat

2¾ cups water, divided

Salt

★ ¼ cup tahini

¼ cup rice vinegar

1 to 2 tablespoons toasted sesame oil, plus more as needed

★ 2 tablespoons finely chopped fresh mint

Freshly ground black pepper

1. In your electric pressure cooker's cooking pot, combine the freekeh, 2½ cups of water, and a pinch of salt. Close and lock the lid and ensure the pressure valve is sealed, then select High Pressure and set the time for 10 minutes (or 5 minutes if using bulgur).

2. When the cook time is complete, let the pressure release naturally for 10 minutes, then quick release any remaining pressure, being careful not to get your fingers or face near the steam release.

3. Meanwhile, in a small bowl, whisk together the remaining ¼ cup of water, tahini, vinegar, sesame oil, and ¼ teaspoon salt until smooth and creamy. Set aside.

4. Once all the pressure has released, carefully unlock and remove the lid. Add the dressing and mint and toss with the freekeh to combine. Taste and season with more salt and pepper and drizzle with more sesame oil, if you like.

PER SERVING Calories: 303; Total fat: 12g; Protein: 9g; Sodium: 172mg; Fiber: 11g

Steel-Cut Oatmeal, 4 Ways

You can make plain steel-cut oatmeal to enjoy with different toppings each day—think nondairy milk, maple syrup or unrefined sugar, fruit, nuts, nut butter, ground flax or chia seeds. Or try one of the three variations listed here to change it up each week! Reheat each portion with some nondairy milk to soften it. *Serves 5*

BUDGET-FRIENDLY, GLUTEN-FREE, NUT-FREE, SOY-FREE

Prep time: 5 minutes · Cooking setting: High Pressure, 10 minutes

Release: Natural for 10 minutes, then Quick; let rest 5 to 10 minutes · Total time: 40 minutes

---

FOR PLAIN OATS

* 1½ cups steel-cut oats

  4 to 5 cups water

  Pinch salt

* 1 cup nondairy milk (optional)

FOR CINNAMON–BROWN SUGAR OATS

* 1 recipe plain oats

  1 teaspoon ground cinnamon

* 1 to 2 tablespoons unrefined sugar or brown sugar

* 1 teaspoon freshly squeezed lemon juice (optional)

FOR APPLE SPICE OATS

* 1 recipe plain oats

* 2 apples, cored and chopped

* 2 tablespoons raisins

  1 teaspoon ground cinnamon

  ¼ teaspoon ground nutmeg

FOR CARROT CAKE OATS

* 1 recipe plain oats

* 2 carrots, scrubbed or peeled and grated

* 1 to 2 tablespoons unrefined sugar, brown sugar, or pure maple syrup

  1 teaspoon ground cinnamon

  ¼ teaspoon ground nutmeg

* ¼ cup chopped walnuts

TO MAKE THE PLAIN OATS

1. In your electric pressure cooker's cooking pot, combine the oats, water (4 cups for a more toothsome oatmeal, 5 cups for a softer porridge), and salt. If you like creamier oats, replace 1 cup of water with nondairy milk. Close and lock the lid and ensure the pressure valve is sealed, then select High Pressure and set the time for 9 to 11 minutes (more time if you like softer oats).

2. When the cook time is complete, let the pressure release naturally for 10 minutes, then quick release any remaining pressure, being careful not to get your fingers or face near the steam release. ➤

3. Once all the pressure has released, carefully unlock and remove the lid. Stir to mix everything together, turn off the pressure cooker, and replace the lid. Let the oats steam for 5 to 10 minutes more. Serve with any toppings you enjoy—nondairy milk, maple syrup or unrefined sugar, fruit, nuts, nut butter, ground flax or chia seeds.

TO MAKE THE CINNAMON-BROWN SUGAR OATS

1. Follow the directions for making plain oats, adding the cinnamon and brown sugar with the oats in step 1.

2. Drizzle the lemon juice on top to serve, if desired.

TO MAKE THE APPLE SPICE OATS

Follow the directions for making plain oats, adding the apples, raisins, cinnamon, and nutmeg with the oats in step 1.

TO MAKE THE CARROT CAKE OATS

Follow the directions for making plain oats, adding the carrots, sugar, cinnamon, and nutmeg with the oats in step 1.

PER SERVING (Plain) Calories: 192; Total fat: 4g; Protein: 7g; Sodium: 0mg; Fiber: 10g

PER SERVING (Cinnamon–Brown Sugar) Calories: 201; Total fat: 4g; Protein: 7g; Sodium: 0mg; Fiber: 10g

PER SERVING (Apple Spice) Calories: 236; Total fat: 4g; Protein: 8g; Sodium: 1mg; Fiber: 11g

PER SERVING (Carrot Cake) Calories: 284; Total fat: 11g; Protein: 9g; Sodium: 18mg; Fiber: 11g

Tip

Cooking plain whole grains gives you ready-made, versatile ingredients to use in different dishes throughout the week. And infusing flavor into them while pressure cooking can make them even tastier. Try adding 1 teaspoon onion powder per 1 cup brown rice, or 1 teaspoon pumpkin pie spice per 1 cup steel-cut oats.

Steel-Cut Oat Milk

Making your own nondairy milk at home is a great way to save money and reduce packaging waste. But the rising prices of cashews and almonds can make you wonder if it's still worthwhile. Oats are really affordable, but you need to cook the oats long enough to be super soft if you want to make milk from them. Enter: electric pressure cooker! *Makes 2 quarts*

BUDGET-FRIENDLY, GLUTEN-FREE, NUT-FREE, SOY-FREE

Prep time: 5 minutes · Cooking setting: High Pressure, 15 minutes
Release: Natural for 10 minutes, then Quick · Total time: 35 minutes

---

* ½ cup steel-cut oats

  8 cups cold water, divided

  Salt

* 2 to 4 tablespoons unrefined sugar (optional)

* 1 teaspoon vanilla extract (optional)

1. In your electric pressure cooker's cooking pot, combine the oats, 4 cups of water, and a pinch of salt. Close and lock the lid and ensure the pressure valve is sealed, then select High Pressure and set the time for 15 minutes.

2. When the cook time is complete, let the pressure release naturally for 10 minutes, then quick release any remaining pressure, being careful not to get your fingers or face near the steam release.

3. Pour the remaining 4 cups of water into a blender.

4. Once all the pressure has released, carefully unlock and remove the lid. Using oven mitts, carefully lift out the pot and transfer the oats to the blender. Purée on high speed for about 1 minute. Depending on the size of your blender, you might have to do this in two batches.

5. Strain the oat mixture through a fine-mesh sieve or nut milk bag into a jar or other airtight container. If you're using sugar or vanilla, stir them in now. Refrigerate for up to 5 days. Shake well before using.

Ingredient tip: You can use the remaining oat fiber in muffins if you like.

PER SERVING (1 cup) Calories: 49; Total fat: 1g; Protein: 2g; Sodium: 0mg; Fiber: 2g

Teriyaki Tempeh
and Broccoli

PAGE 42

CHAPTER 3

Basic Beans and Legumes

Cooking dried beans and legumes on the stovetop uses a significant amount of electricity (or gas). With an electric pressure cooker, beans require much less electricity and time. Even better, you don't have to watch the pot to make sure it doesn't boil over, so you can do other things while they cook.

Vegans need to include beans and legumes in their diet to make sure they get enough of the amino acid lysine, which is also available from whole grains and some other plant foods, but in insufficient concentration to meet daily needs within a reasonable calorie intake.

Spice It Up!

You'll find recipes in this chapter to make delicious meals with beans and legumes, but the simplest way to get started is to simply cook a batch of beans with some spices. The pressure will infuse the beans with flavor, and you can then simply toss them into a salad or soup on the fly. Try adding 1 teaspoon smoked paprika or ground cinnamon to every 1 cup chickpeas, 1 teaspoon chili powder to every 1 cup black beans, or 1 tablespoon dried basil to every 1 cup white beans.

Easy on Your Wallet

Beans and legumes are cheaper per gram of protein than beef, eggs, or fish. You can save even more money by buying dried beans and legumes rather than canned, but the savings could get used up in the energy required to cook them on the stovetop. However, the dried variety will help you cut back on sodium and avoid BPA.

Taco/Burrito Filling

This simply seasoned black bean recipe can be used as a filling for tacos or burritos or served in a bowl with Cilantro-Lime Brown and Wild Rice (page 20). The beans cook up just soft enough to add some texture to your tacos. If you want softer beans for bowls, include an extra ½ cup broth and add 5 minutes to the time at pressure. *Serves 4 to 6*

BUDGET-FRIENDLY, GLUTEN-FREE, NUT-FREE, SOY-FREE

Prep time: 5 minutes · Cooking setting: High Pressure, 30 minutes · Release: Natural · Total time: 1 hour

---

2 cups water or unsalted vegetable broth

★ 1 cup dried black beans

2 to 3 tablespoons chili powder

1 tablespoon olive oil (optional)

2 teaspoons onion powder

1 teaspoon garlic powder

1 teaspoon smoked paprika *or* 1 more teaspoon chili powder

1 teaspoon ground cumin (optional)

¼ to ½ teaspoon salt

1. In your electric pressure cooker's cooking pot, combine the water, black beans, chili powder, olive oil (if using), onion powder, garlic powder, paprika, and cumin (if using). Close and lock the lid and ensure the pressure valve is sealed, then select High Pressure and set the time for 30 minutes.

2. Once the cook time is complete, release the pressure naturally for about 25 minutes.

3. Once all the pressure has released, carefully unlock and remove the lid. Add the salt. If the beans are not quite soft enough, or if you have too much liquid, select Sauté or Simmer and cook them, uncovered, for 15 to 20 minutes more.

Preparation tip: The oil is optional but highly recommended because it helps carry the spices and minimizes foaming of the beans.

PER SERVING Calories: 217; Total fat: 5g; Protein: 12g; Sodium: 186mg; Fiber: 13g

Curried Lentils

Here's a simple, delicious, and highly nutritious dish you can make in a pressure cooker any night of the week, year-round. Serve it with cooked couscous, quinoa, or Cilantro-Lime Brown and Wild Rice (page 20), plus steamed or sautéed veggies and maybe some warmed naan. No need for takeout! *Serves 4*

BUDGET-FRIENDLY, GLUTEN-FREE, NUT-FREE, SOY-FREE

Prep time: 5 minutes · Cooking setting: Sauté, 1 minute, then High Pressure, 20 minutes

Release: Natural · Total time: 1 hour

---

1 tablespoon coconut oil

2 tablespoons mild curry powder

1 teaspoon ground ginger

½ teaspoon ground turmeric (optional)

★ 1 cup dried green lentils or brown lentils

3 cups water

★ 1 teaspoon freshly squeezed lime juice (optional)

½ teaspoon salt

Freshly ground black pepper (optional)

1. On your electric pressure cooker, select Sauté. Add the coconut oil, curry powder, ginger, and turmeric (if using) and toss to toast for 1 minute. Add the lentils and toss with the spices. Add the water. Cancel Sauté.

2. Close and lock the lid and ensure the pressure valve is sealed, then select High Pressure and set the time for 20 minutes.

3. Once the cook time is complete, let the pressure release naturally, about 30 minutes.

4. Once all the pressure has released, carefully unlock and remove the lid. Stir in the lime juice (if using). Season with the salt and pepper, if you like.

PER SERVING Calories: 212; Total fat: 5g; Protein: 13g; Sodium: 2mg; Fiber: 16g

Coconut Curry Tofu

Serve this super flavorful curry over brown rice, along with warmed naan or pita to soak up all the flavorful sauce. While pressure cooking doesn't save time with tofu, it does help infuse the flavor into the tofu much better than cooking on the stovetop. *Serves 4*

GLUTEN-FREE, NUT-FREE

Prep time: 5 minutes · Cooking setting: High Pressure, 3 minutes · Release: Quick · Total time: 15 minutes

★ 1 (13.5-ounce) can coconut milk

★ ¼ cup red or green curry paste

¼ teaspoon salt, plus more as needed

¼ cup water

★ 1 (14-ounce) package firm or extra-firm tofu, pressed and cubed

★ 2 teaspoons unrefined sugar or brown sugar

★ 2 cups chopped fresh spinach

1. In your electric pressure cooker's cooking pot, combine the coconut milk, curry paste, salt, and water, stirring to combine. Add the tofu. Close and lock the lid and ensure the pressure valve is sealed, then select High Pressure and set the time for 3 minutes.

2. Once the cook time is complete, quick release the pressure, being careful not to get your fingers or face near the steam release.

3. Once all the pressure has released, carefully unlock and remove the lid. Stir in the sugar and spinach. Taste and season with more salt, if needed.

Preparation tip: Add whatever vegetables you like—cook some carrots, red bell pepper, or onion with the tofu, or stir in a handful of frozen corn or peas with the spinach and cook until they are heated through.

PER SERVING Calories: 438; Total fat: 36g; Protein: 13g; Sodium: 169mg; Fiber: 4g

Chipotle Chickpeas

These chipotle-infused chickpeas pair perfectly with creamy guacamole. They also make a great taco filling or component of a Buddha bowl with cooked rice or quinoa, your choice of fresh veggies, vegan cheese, and lime juice. You can even bake them (at 350°F for 30 to 45 minutes) and enjoy as a crunchy snack. *Serves 4 to 6*

BUDGET-FRIENDLY, GLUTEN-FREE, NUT-FREE, SOY-FREE

Prep time: 8 minutes, or overnight · Cooking setting: High Pressure, 20 minutes
Release: Natural · Total time: 45 minutes, plus soaking

★ 1 cup dried chickpeas, soaked in water overnight or quick soaked for 8 minutes on High Pressure

2 cups water

★ ¼ cup sun-dried tomatoes, chopped

1 to 2 tablespoons olive oil

★ 2 teaspoons ground chipotle pepper

1½ teaspoons ground cumin

1½ teaspoons onion powder

1 teaspoon dried oregano

¾ teaspoon garlic powder

½ teaspoon smoked paprika

¼ to ½ teaspoon salt

1. Drain and rinse the chickpeas, drain again, and put them in your electric pressure cooker's cooking pot.

2. Add the water, sun-dried tomatoes, olive oil, chipotle pepper, cumin, onion powder, oregano, garlic powder, and paprika. Close and lock the lid and ensure the pressure valve is sealed, then select High Pressure and set the time for 20 minutes.

3. Once the cook time is complete, let the pressure release naturally, about 15 minutes.

4. Once all the pressure has released, carefully unlock and remove the lid. Taste and season with salt and more oil or seasonings if you like.

Preparation tip: If you forget to soak your chickpeas overnight, you can quick soak them in the pressure cooker: In your electric pressure cooker's cooking pot, combine the chickpeas with plenty of water (3 to 4 cups). Close and lock the lid and ensure the pressure valve is sealed, then select High Pressure and set the time for 8 minutes. Once the cook time is complete, let the pressure release naturally, about 20 minutes.

Ingredient tip: If you can't find ground chipotle pepper in the spice section of your grocery store, substitute 1 teaspoon chili powder plus 1 more teaspoon smoked paprika.

PER SERVING Calories: 280; Total fat: 7g; Protein: 13g; Sodium: 168mg; Fiber: 12g

Cinnamon Chickpeas

Here's a different spin on chickpeas—sweet! When they're super soft and cooked without salt in your electric pressure cooker, they take on a whole new persona. Serve with chopped pear or scattered over Sweet Potato Breakfast Bowls (page 74) for a protein boost to your breakfast, or toss them in a salad with chopped grapes, walnuts, and a raspberry-balsamic vinaigrette for a tasty, light lunch. Note that these are not crispy like roasted chickpea snacks, but rather soft and creamy. *Serves 4 to 6*

BUDGET-FRIENDLY, GLUTEN-FREE, NUT-FREE, SOY-FREE

Prep time: 8 minutes, or overnight · Cooking setting: High Pressure, 30 minutes, then Sauté, 5 minutes
Release: Natural · Total time: 50 minutes, plus soaking

★ 1 cup dried chickpeas, soaked in water overnight or quick soaked for 8 minutes on High Pressure (see tip in the recipe for Chipotle Chickpeas, page 37)

2 cups water

2 teaspoons ground cinnamon, plus more as needed

½ teaspoon ground nutmeg (optional)

1 tablespoon coconut oil

★ 2 to 4 tablespoons unrefined sugar or brown sugar, plus more as needed

1. Drain and rinse the chickpeas, then put them in your electric pressure cooker's cooking pot.

2. Add the water, cinnamon, and nutmeg (if using). Close and lock the lid and ensure the pressure valve is sealed, then select High Pressure and set the time for 30 minutes.

3. Once the cook time is complete, let the pressure release naturally, about 15 minutes.

4. Once all the pressure has released, carefully unlock and remove the lid. Drain any excess water from the chickpeas and add them back to the pot.

5. Stir in the coconut oil and sugar. Taste and add more cinnamon, if desired. Select Sauté and cook for about 5 minutes, stirring the chickpeas occasionally, until there's no liquid left and the sugar has melted onto the chickpeas. Transfer to a bowl and toss with additional sugar if you want to add a crunchy texture.

Variation tip: Squeeze fresh lime or lemon juice over these for a taste sensation.

PER SERVING Calories: 253; Total fat: 7g; Protein: 11g; Sodium: 9mg; Fiber: 10g

Black-Eyed Peas and Collard Greens

This recipe pairs black-eyed peas and collard greens, two quintessentially Southern dishes. Try it with some pressure-cooked quinoa or rice. *Serves 4 to 6*

BUDGET-FRIENDLY, GLUTEN-FREE, NUT-FREE, SOY-FREE

Prep time: 5 minutes · Cooking setting: Sauté, 3 to 4 minutes, then High Pressure, 30 minutes
Release: Natural · Total time: 55 minutes

★ 1 yellow onion, diced

　1 tablespoon olive oil

★ 1 cup dried black-eyed peas

　2 cups water or unsalted vegetable broth

★ ¼ cup chopped sun-dried tomatoes

★ ¼ cup tomato paste or natural ketchup

　1 teaspoon smoked paprika

　Pinch red pepper flakes (optional)

★ 4 large collard green leaves

　Salt

　Freshly ground black pepper

1. On your electric pressure cooker, select Sauté. Add the onion and olive oil and cook for 3 to 4 minutes, stirring occasionally, until the onion is softened. Add the black-eyed peas, water, tomatoes, tomato paste, paprika, and red pepper flakes (if using) and stir to combine. Cancel Sauté.

2. Close and lock the lid and ensure the pressure valve is sealed, then select High Pressure and set the time for 30 minutes.

3. Once the cook time is complete, let the pressure release naturally, about 15 minutes.

4. Trim off the thick parts of the collard green stems, then slice the leaves lengthwise in half or quarters (depending on how large the leaves are). Roll them up together, then finely slice into ribbons. Sprinkle the sliced collard greens with a pinch of salt and massage it into them with your hands to soften.

5. Once all the pressure has released, carefully unlock and remove the lid. Add the collard greens and ½ teaspoon of salt to the pot, stirring to combine and letting the greens wilt in the heat. Taste and season with salt and pepper. If you want your greens cooked more, select Sauté again for another few minutes.

PER SERVING Calories: 267; Total fat: 5g; Protein: 15g; Sodium: 332mg; Fiber: 13g

Lentil Bolognese Sauce

The electric pressure cooker makes it easy to whip together a hearty and protein-rich sauce for spaghetti—or spaghetti squash! Mushrooms add a deep, savory flavor to this meatless sauce, but if you're cooking for palates that don't enjoy mushrooms, you can omit the mushrooms and use a mushroom-based vegetable broth for at least 1 cup of the liquid. If you have some on hand, adding about ½ cup of tomato paste along with the crushed tomatoes really boosts the flavor. *Makes 3 cups*

BUDGET-FRIENDLY, GLUTEN-FREE, NUT-FREE, SOY-FREE

Prep time: 10 minutes · Cooking setting: Sauté, 10 minutes, then High Pressure, 10 minutes
Release: Natural · Total time: 50 minutes

---

* ★ 12 ounces mushrooms, sliced (about 4½ cups)
* ★ 1 onion, diced
* 1 tablespoon olive oil or vegan margarine
* ★ ½ cup dry white wine or red wine
* ★ 2 cups dried green lentils or brown lentils
* ★ 1 (28-ounce) can crushed tomatoes
* 2 cups water or unsalted vegetable broth
* ¼ to ½ teaspoon salt
* Freshly ground black pepper

1. On your electric pressure cooker, select Sauté. Add the mushrooms, onion, and olive oil and toss to combine. Cover the pot but do not lock the lid, and cook for 7 to 8 minutes, until the onion and mushrooms are slightly browned. Add the wine and cook for 1 to 2 minutes more until evaporated.

2. Stir in the lentils, tomatoes, and water. Cancel Sauté.

3. Close and lock the lid and ensure the pressure valve is sealed, then select High Pressure and set the time for 10 minutes.

4. Once the cook time is complete, let the pressure release naturally, about 20 minutes.

5. Once all the pressure has released, carefully unlock and remove the lid. Taste and season with salt and pepper

---

Ingredient tip: Add extra veggies along with the mushrooms and onion, such as chopped carrot and celery, which are typical for a Bolognese sauce. Fresh parsley stirred through at the end adds a huge nutritional boost and a splash of color.

PER SERVING (½ cup) Calories: 303; Total fat: 4g; Protein: 19g; Sodium: 114mg; Fiber: 21g

Feijoada

This Brazilian black bean stew traditionally contains meat, but we're going to make a vegan version and bump up the flavor with smoked paprika. Brazilian families enjoy this for a long Sunday afternoon feast, along with caipirinhas, and then they fall into a blissful afternoon nap. *Serves 6 to 8*

BUDGET-FRIENDLY, GLUTEN-FREE, NUT-FREE, SOY-FREE

Prep time: 10 minutes · Cooking setting: Sauté, 5 minutes, then High Pressure, 30 minutes

Release: Natural · Total time: 1 hour, 15 minutes

- ★ 1 large onion, diced
- ★ 3 or 4 garlic cloves, minced
- 1 tablespoon olive oil
- ★ 2 cups dried black beans
- 4 cups water and/or unsalted vegetable broth
- 1 tablespoon ground cumin
- 1 tablespoon smoked paprika
- 1 tablespoon dried oregano
- Salt
- ★ ¼ cup fresh cilantro, chopped

1. On your electric pressure cooker, select Sauté. Add the onion, garlic, and olive oil. Cook for about 5 minutes, stirring occasionally, until the onion is softened. Add the black beans, water, cumin, paprika, and oregano, stirring to combine. Cancel Sauté.

2. Close and lock the lid and ensure the pressure valve is sealed, then select High Pressure and set the time for 30 minutes.

3. When the cook time is complete, let the pressure release naturally, about 30 minutes.

4. Once all the pressure has released, carefully unlock and remove the lid. Taste and season with ½ to 1 teaspoon of salt. If your beans are not quite soft enough, or if you have too much liquid, select Sauté or Simmer and cook, uncovered, for 10 to 15 minutes more. Stir in the cilantro just before serving.

Serving tip: Serve with rice, sautéed collard greens or kale, and orange wedges. For an authentic cultural experience, toast ½ cup cassava flour in 2 to 3 tablespoons coconut oil in a small skillet over medium heat for 3 to 5 minutes until browned; sprinkle over the finished dish.

PER SERVING Calories: 268; Total fat: 4g; Protein: 16g; Sodium: 199mg; Fiber: 16g

Teriyaki Tempeh and Broccoli

Tempeh is made of soy but is totally different from tofu. It's a dense patty of cultured soybeans that originated in Indonesia. Like tofu, tempeh needs to have flavor infused into it and also needs to be cooked. Putting it in the electric pressure cooker with bold flavors is a perfect way to quickly create an irresistible meal. *Serves 2*

NUT-FREE

Prep time: 10 minutes · Cooking setting: High Pressure, 5 minutes · Release: Quick · Total time: 20 minutes

---

★ ¼ cup tamari or soy sauce

¼ cup water

1 tablespoon olive oil or untoasted sesame oil

★ 1 tablespoon pure maple syrup or unrefined sugar

★ 1 teaspoon cornstarch or arrowroot powder

½ teaspoon ground ginger *or* 1 teaspoon grated peeled fresh ginger

★ 1 (8- or 9-ounce) package tempeh, cubed

★ ½ head broccoli, cut into pieces

1. In your electric pressure cooker's cooking pot, stir together the tamari, water, olive oil, maple syrup, cornstarch, and ginger. Add the tempeh and broccoli (or put the broccoli in a steamer basket on a trivet to cook above the tempeh, if you like). Close and lock the lid and ensure the pressure valve is sealed, then select High Pressure and set the time for 5 minutes.

2. When the cook time is complete, quick release the pressure, being careful not to get your fingers or face near the steam release.

3. Once all the pressure has released, carefully unlock and remove the lid and toss to combine.

Serving tip: For a complete meal, serve this dish with cooked quinoa or Cilantro-Lime Brown and Wild Rice (page 20), sprinkled with toasted sesame seeds or cashews. Try garnishing the dish with sliced scallions.

PER SERVING Calories: 336; Total fat: 18g; Protein: 25g; Sodium: 2g; Fiber: 3g

Tofu Feta

While making tofu feta is a fairly simple procedure—marinating tofu with vinegar and seasonings—preparing it in the electric pressure cooker takes a lot less time. It makes a great addition to salads or pasta dishes. ***Serves 6 to 8***

BUDGET-FRIENDLY, NUT-FREE

Prep time: 5 minutes · Cooking setting: High Pressure, 10 minutes · Release: Quick · Total time: 25 minutes

---

¼ cup red wine vinegar

★ 2 tablespoons freshly squeezed lemon juice

★ 2 tablespoons red or white miso paste

2 tablespoons olive oil

1 teaspoon garlic powder

1 teaspoon salt

★ 1 (14-ounce) package extra-firm tofu, cubed

1. In a heat-proof dish that fits inside your electric pressure cooker's cooking pot, stir together the vinegar, lemon juice, miso, olive oil, garlic powder, and salt until smooth. Add the tofu cubes, tossing to coat.

2. Put a trivet in the pot and pour in a cup or two of water. Put the dish on top of the trivet. If it's a tight fit, use an aluminum foil sling or silicone helper handles (see page 5).

3. Close and lock the lid and ensure the pressure valve is sealed, then select High Pressure and set the time for 10 minutes.

4. When the cook time is complete, quick release the pressure, being careful not to get your fingers or face near the steam release.

5. Once all the pressure has released, carefully unlock and remove the lid. Let cool for a few minutes before carefully lifting out the dish with oven mitts or tongs. Refrigerate the tofu in an airtight container with the marinade, then strain it to serve.

PER SERVING Calories: 176; Total fat: 12g; Protein: 14g; Sodium: 562mg; Fiber: 2g

Smoky Corn and
Squash Chowder

PAGE 52

CHAPTER 4

Soups, Stews, and Chilis

Using your electric pressure cooker to make soups, stews, and chilis results in the same rich, rounded flavor you get from slow cooking, but in a much shorter time. That means you also save energy! The flavors are comparable, but you keep more of the texture—and nutrients—of the foods in your dish.

Spice It Up!

The base of many good soups is onion plus garlic or ginger. After that, seasonings are the key to making soups with different flavors to keep your taste buds intrigued. Some people like more seasoning and spice than others. Personally, I like a lot of seasoning but not a ton of spice. If you find you need more kick to any of these soups, try a pinch of cayenne or red pepper flakes. The best approach with seasoning is to start small, because you can always add more—but you can't take it out.

Thai Coconut-Chickpea Stew

This creamy, flavorful soup will spice up any evening. You can switch up the vegetables if you prefer—try carrots or cauliflower. Squeeze in some lime juice at the end for an added flavor pop, and if you have some fresh cilantro or Thai basil, chop some and sprinkle it on top before serving. *Serves 4 to 5*

BUDGET-FRIENDLY, NUT-FREE

Prep time: 10 minutes · Cooking setting: High Pressure, 3 minutes
Release: Natural or Quick · Total time: 20 to 35 minutes

---

* 8 ounces mushrooms, sliced (about 3 cups)

* 3 cups cooked chickpeas (from 1 cup dried)

* 1 red bell pepper, seeded and chopped

* 1 (13.5-ounce) can coconut milk

* 2 tablespoons tamari or soy sauce

  1 teaspoon Thai chili paste

  1 teaspoon ground ginger

  Salt

1. In your electric pressure cooker's cooking pot, combine the mushrooms, chickpeas, red bell pepper, coconut milk, tamari, chili paste, and ginger. Close and lock the lid and ensure the pressure valve is sealed, then select High Pressure and set the time for 3 minutes.

2. Once the cook time is complete, let the pressure release naturally, about 20 minutes, or quick release it, being careful not to get your fingers or face near the steam release.

3. Once all the pressure has released, carefully unlock and remove the lid. Taste and season with salt.

Preparation tip: You'll want to cook the chickpeas in advance, since they take so much longer than the other ingredients. I like to cook a big batch of one or two plain beans for the week, which I can then throw into salads or soups like this. Just put the dried chickpeas in your electric pressure cooker's cooking pot with plenty of water to cover, and cook on High Pressure for 30 minutes.

PER SERVING Calories: 400; Total fat: 21g; Protein: 15g; Sodium: 277mg; Fiber: 11g

Black Bean, Pumpkin, and Kale Chili

Rich and satisfying, a hearty chili is the perfect meal for a winter's night. Black beans are an excellent source of folate, which is crucial for the health of the brain and nervous system, as well as cardiovascular health. Black beans also cook a lot faster than kidney beans and may not cause as much of the notorious gas associated with chili. Top this off with some guacamole or chopped avocado and a scoop of vegan sour cream. *Serves 4 to 5*

BUDGET-FRIENDLY, GLUTEN-FREE, NUT-FREE, SOY-FREE

Prep time: 8 minutes, or overnight · Cooking setting: High Pressure, 10 minutes
Release: Natural · Total time: 30 minutes, plus soaking

★ ¾ cup dried black beans, soaked in water overnight or quick soaked for 8 minutes on High Pressure (see tip, page 37), drained

★ 1 (28-ounce) can crushed tomatoes

★ 2 cups chopped pumpkin

2 to 3 cups water or unsalted vegetable broth

2 tablespoons chili powder

1 teaspoon onion powder

½ teaspoon garlic powder

★ 2 to 3 cups finely shredded kale

½ teaspoon salt

1. Drain the black beans, then put them in your electric pressure cooker's cooking pot.

2. Add the tomatoes, pumpkin, water (2 cups for thick chili, 3 cups if you like it a bit more soupy), chili powder, onion powder, and garlic powder. Close and lock the lid and ensure the pressure valve is sealed, then select High Pressure and set the time for 10 minutes.

3. Once the cook time is complete, let the pressure release naturally, about 20 minutes.

4. Once all the pressure has released, carefully unlock and remove the lid. Stir in the kale to wilt. Stir in the salt.

Make-ahead tip: This is a great recipe to double-batch and freeze in single (or family) servings for easy weeknight meals.

PER SERVING Calories: 209; Total fat: 2g; Protein: 13g; Sodium: 363mg; Fiber: 13g

Leek and Potato Soup

Potatoes are often underestimated nutritionally, but they're a good source of vitamins C and B_6, potassium, and fiber, and they contain a natural compound that may help lower blood pressure. Here, potatoes costar with leeks in a deliciously creamy and savory soup. *Serves 5 to 6*

GLUTEN-FREE, NUT-FREE, SOY-FREE

Prep time: 10 minutes · Cooking setting: Sauté, 4 to 5 minutes, then High Pressure, 7 minutes
Release: Natural · Total time: 45 minutes

- ✱ 3 leeks (white and light green parts only), chopped
- ✱ 1 white or yellow onion, chopped
- ✱ 3 or 4 garlic cloves, minced
- 1 tablespoon olive oil
- ✱ 6 medium russet potatoes, scrubbed or peeled and roughly chopped (6 to 7 cups)
- ✱ ½ (13.5-ounce) can coconut milk (about ¾ cup)
- 4 cups water or unsalted vegetable broth
- ½ teaspoon salt, plus more as needed
- 1 teaspoon garlic powder (optional)
- Freshly ground black pepper

1. On your electric pressure cooker, select Sauté. Add the leeks, onion, garlic, and olive oil. Cook for 4 to 5 minutes, stirring occasionally, until the leek and onion are softened.

2. Add the potatoes, coconut milk, water, and salt. Cancel Sauté.

3. Close and lock the lid and ensure the pressure valve is sealed, then select High Pressure and set the time for 7 minutes.

4. Once the cook time is complete, let the pressure release naturally, about 20 minutes.

5. Once all the pressure has released, carefully unlock and remove the lid. Let cool for a few minutes and then purée the soup—either use an immersion blender right in the pot or transfer the soup (in batches, if necessary) to a countertop blender. Taste and season with the garlic powder (if using), salt, and pepper.

Ingredient tip: To clean leeks, cut off the root ends and trim away the dark green leaves, then halve the leeks lengthwise. Thoroughly wash inside all the folds, as dirt likes to hide there.

PER SERVING Calories: 274; Total fat: 10g; Protein: 5g; Sodium: 248mg; Fiber: 4g

Split Pea Soup

This hearty soup is full of plant protein from the peas. The sun-dried tomatoes (or olives, if you prefer) add a pop of savory flavor to replace the typical ham that would be included in this soup. Don't use canned olives, though, as their flavor is usually diluted. Instead, buy a jar of whole pitted olives, then chop them. If you like, stir in a tablespoon or two of nutritional yeast before serving. *Serves 6*

BUDGET-FRIENDLY, NUT-FREE

Prep time: 10 minutes · Cooking setting: High Pressure, 10 minutes · Release: Natural · Total time: 45 minutes

---

★ 3 or 4 carrots, scrubbed or peeled and chopped

★ 1 large yellow onion, chopped

★ 1 cup dried split green peas

3 cups water or unsalted vegetable broth

★ 1 tablespoon tamari or soy sauce

2 to 3 teaspoons dried thyme *or* 1 teaspoon ground thyme

1 teaspoon onion powder

½ teaspoon garlic powder

Pinch freshly ground black pepper

★ ¼ cup chopped sun-dried tomatoes or chopped pitted black olives

Salt

1. In your electric pressure cooker's cooking pot, combine the carrots, onion, split peas, water, tamari, thyme, onion powder, garlic powder, and pepper. Close and lock the lid and ensure the pressure valve is sealed, then select High Pressure and set the time for 10 minutes.

2. Once the cook time is complete, let the pressure release naturally, about 20 minutes.

3. Once all the pressure has released, carefully unlock and remove the lid. Let cool for a few minutes and then purée the soup—either use an immersion blender right in the pot or transfer the soup (in batches, if necessary) to a countertop blender.

4. Stir in the nutritional yeast (if using) and sun-dried tomatoes. Taste and season with salt.

Serving tip: Serve topped with chopped fresh cherry tomatoes and scallion, with a fresh green salad alongside.

PER SERVING Calories: 182; Total fat: 1g; Protein: 12g; Sodium: 301mg; Fiber: 12g

Vegetable and Barley Stew

This is a perfect meal for those days when you just want to throw a bunch of things in a pot and let it simmer while you wind down. Except, in this case, simmering under pressure means dinner's ready in 20 minutes instead of an hour. *Serves 4 to 5*

BUDGET-FRIENDLY, NUT-FREE, SOY-FREE

Prep time: 15 minutes · Cooking setting: High Pressure, 20 minutes · Release: Quick · Total time: 45 minutes

---

★ 2 or 3 parsnips, peeled and chopped

★ 2 cups chopped peeled sweet potato, russet potato, winter squash, or pumpkin

★ 1 large yellow onion, chopped

★ 1 cup pearl barley

★ 1 (28-ounce) can diced tomatoes

4 cups water or unsalted vegetable broth

2 to 3 teaspoons dried mixed herbs *or* 1 teaspoon dried basil plus 1 teaspoon dried oregano

Salt

Freshly ground black pepper

1. In your electric pressure cooker's cooking pot, combine the parsnips, sweet potato, onion, barley, tomatoes with their juice, water, and herbs. Close and lock the lid and ensure the pressure valve is sealed, then select High Pressure and set the time for 20 minutes.

2. Once the cook time is complete, quick release the pressure, being careful not to get your fingers or face near the steam release.

3. Once all the pressure has released, carefully unlock and remove the lid. Taste and season with salt and pepper.

Make-ahead tip: Save yourself time later in the week (or month) by making a double batch and freezing some in single (or family) servings.

PER SERVING Calories: 300; Total fat: 2g; Protein: 9g; Sodium: 209mg; Fiber: 14g

Sweet Potato and Peanut Stew

This sweet, creamy stew has a bit of a kick to it. If you don't like things spicy, start with just a pinch of red pepper flakes or cayenne. You can always add more after cooking—or leave it out entirely! Or, instead of spice, you could stir in a bit of freshly squeezed lime or lemon juice after cooking to brighten the flavors. *Serves 4*

BUDGET-FRIENDLY, GLUTEN-FREE, SOY-FREE

Prep time: 10 minutes · Cooking setting: Sauté, 4 to 5 minutes, then High Pressure, 6 minutes
Release: Quick · Total time: 30 minutes

★ 2 onions, diced

2 tablespoons olive oil or coconut oil

★ 2 large sweet potatoes, peeled and chopped (about 4 cups)

★ ⅓ cup chunky peanut butter

1 teaspoon smoked paprika

¼ teaspoon red pepper flakes *or* ⅛ teaspoon cayenne

2 cups water or unsalted vegetable broth

¼ teaspoon salt, plus more as needed

★ 1 to 2 cups finely chopped fresh spinach or kale

Freshly ground black pepper

1. On your electric pressure cooker select Sauté. Add the onions and olive oil and cook for 4 to 5 minutes, stirring occasionally, until the onion is softened. Stir in the sweet potatoes, peanut butter, paprika, red pepper flakes, water, and salt. Stir to mix the peanut butter into the water a bit, but don't worry too much, as it will melt when heated. Cancel Sauté.

2. Close and lock the lid and ensure the pressure valve is sealed, then select High Pressure and set the time for 6 minutes.

3. Once the cook time is complete, quick release the pressure, being careful not to get your fingers or face near the steam release.

4. Once all the pressure has released, carefully unlock and remove the lid. Stir in the spinach to wilt. Taste and season with more salt and pepper.

Ingredient tip: Either orange- or white-fleshed sweet potatoes work well in this soup.

PER SERVING Calories: 350; Total fat: 18g; Protein: 10g; Sodium: 240mg; Fiber: 8g

Smoky Corn and Squash Chowder

A little smoked paprika adds depth to this chowder, which gets a vitamin A and C boost from squash or sweet potatoes. *Serves 4 to 5*

BUDGET-FRIENDLY, GLUTEN-FREE, NUT-FREE, SOY-FREE

Prep time: 10 minutes · Cooking setting: Sauté, 4 to 5 minutes, then High Pressure, 5 minutes

Release: Quick · Total time: 30 minutes

- ★ 1 onion, chopped
- ★ 2 garlic cloves, chopped
-   1 teaspoon olive oil
- ★ 1 butternut squash or 2 sweet potatoes, peeled and chopped
-   2 cups water
- ★ 2 cups unsalted vegetable broth
-   1 teaspoon smoked paprika
-   ½ teaspoon salt, plus more as needed
-   Pinch freshly ground black pepper, plus more as needed
- ★ 4 cups fresh or frozen corn
-   Chopped scallion, for garnish (optional)

1. On your electric pressure cooker, select Sauté. Add the onion, garlic, and olive oil. Cook for 4 to 5 minutes, stirring occasionally, until the onion is softened. Add the squash, water, vegetable broth, paprika, salt, and pepper. Cancel Sauté.

2. Close and lock the lid and ensure the pressure valve is sealed, then select High Pressure and set the time for 5 minutes.

3. Once the cook time is complete, quick release the pressure, being careful not to get your fingers or face near the steam release.

4. Once all the pressure has released, carefully unlock and remove the lid. Add the corn to the pot and let it heat through. Purée about half of the soup, or as much as you like—either use an immersion blender right in the pot or scoop out some of the squash and corn and let it cool for a few minutes before puréeing in a countertop blender. Taste and season with more salt and pepper, if needed, and top with chopped scallion.

Preparation tip: If you're pressed for time, skip the sauté step and just put the onion and garlic in with the rest of the ingredients. The chowder won't have quite as rich a flavor, but you might not even notice.

PER SERVING Calories: 219; Total fat: 2g; Protein: 6g; Sodium: 298mg; Fiber: 7g

Golden Carrot and Cauliflower Soup

Full of antioxidants from cauliflower and anti-inflammatory compounds from the ginger and turmeric, this is one powerfully healthy soup. It also happens to be incredibly delicious! *Serves 4 to 5*

BUDGET-FRIENDLY, GLUTEN-FREE, NUT-FREE, SOY-FREE

Prep time: 10 minutes · Cooking setting: Sauté, 4 to 5 minutes, then High Pressure, 7 minutes

Release: Natural · Total time: 50 minutes

* 1 onion, chopped

* 1 tablespoon minced peeled fresh ginger *or* 1 teaspoon ground ginger

  1 teaspoon olive oil

* 5 or 6 carrots, scrubbed or peeled and chopped

* 1 head cauliflower, chopped into florets

* ½ (13.5-ounce) can coconut milk (about ¾ cup)

  3 cups water or unsalted vegetable broth

  ½ teaspoon ground turmeric

  ¼ to ½ teaspoon salt, plus more as needed

  Freshly ground black pepper

1. On your electric pressure cooker, select Sauté. Add the onion, ginger, and olive oil. Cook for 4 to 5 minutes, stirring occasionally, until the onion is softened. Add the carrots, cauliflower, coconut milk, water, turmeric, and salt. Cancel Sauté.

2. Close and lock the lid and ensure the pressure valve is sealed, then select High Pressure and set the time for 7 minutes.

3. Once the cook time is complete, let the pressure release naturally, about 20 minutes.

4. Once all the pressure has released, carefully unlock and remove the lid. Let cool for a few minutes and then purée the soup—either use an immersion blender right in the pot or transfer it (in batches, if necessary) to a countertop blender. Taste and season with more salt and pepper, if needed.

Ingredient tip: If you have fresh turmeric, mince 1 teaspoon and sauté it with the onion and ginger.

PER SERVING Calories: 176; Total fat: 11g; Protein: 4g; Sodium: 249mg; Fiber: 6g

Sweet and Spicy Chickpea Stew

This is a really fun and flavorful stew with Moroccan-inspired ingredients, including olives, apricots, curry powder, and cinnamon. Top off the stew with a sprinkle of sesame seeds if you like, plus some chopped fresh parsley or mint for a burst of green. *Serves 4 to 6*

BUDGET-FRIENDLY, GLUTEN-FREE, NUT-FREE, SOY-FREE

Prep time: 10 minutes · Cooking setting: High Pressure, 5 minutes · Release: Natural or Quick · Total time: 35 minutes

---

★ 3 cups cooked chickpeas (from 1 cup dried)

2 cups water or vegetable broth

★ 2 or 3 carrots, scrubbed or peeled and chopped

★ 1 (28-ounce) can diced tomatoes

★ ¼ cup chopped green olives

★ ¼ cup chopped dried apricots

1 tablespoon unrefined sugar or brown sugar

2 teaspoons curry powder

1 teaspoon ground cinnamon

½ teaspoon salt, plus more as needed

Freshly ground black pepper

1. In your electric pressure cooker's cooking pot, combine the chickpeas, water or vegetable broth, carrots, tomatoes with their juice, olives, apricots, sugar, curry powder, cinnamon, and salt. Season with pepper. Close and lock the lid and ensure the pressure valve is sealed, then select High Pressure and set the time for 5 minutes.

2. Once the cook time is complete, let the pressure release naturally, about 20 minutes or quick release it, being careful not to get your fingers or face near the steam release.

3. Once all the pressure has released, carefully unlock and remove the lid. Taste and season with more salt, if needed, and pepper.

PER SERVING Calories: 327; Total fat: 6g; Protein: 14g; Sodium: 402mg; Fiber: 15g

Miso, Mushroom, and Red Lentil Stew

This rich, savory stew is full of protein from the red lentils. It's fantastic on its own, or you can pair it with some cooked whole grains and steamed veggies for a lunch bowl to pack up for the week. *Serves 4*

BUDGET-FRIENDLY, NUT-FREE

Prep time: 5 minutes · Cooking setting: Sauté, 6 to 7 minutes, then High Pressure, 3 minutes
Release: Quick · Total time: 25 minutes

★ 1 red onion, thinly sliced

★ 8 ounces shiitake mushrooms or cremini mushrooms, sliced (about 2½ cups)

1 to 2 teaspoons toasted sesame oil

Salt

★ 1 (1-inch) piece fresh ginger, peeled and minced

★ 1 cup dried red lentils

4 cups water and/or unsalted vegetable broth

★ 2 to 3 tablespoons red or white miso paste

Freshly ground black pepper

1. On your electric pressure cooker, select Sauté. Add the red onion, mushrooms, sesame oil, and a pinch of salt. Cook for 6 to 7 minutes, stirring occasionally, until the vegetables are softened. Add the ginger in the last minute or two of cooking.

2. Add the lentils and water to the pot. Cancel Sauté.

3. Close and lock the lid and ensure the pressure valve is sealed, then select High Pressure and set the time for 3 minutes.

4. Once the cook time is complete, quick release the pressure, being careful not to get your fingers or face near the steam release.

5. Once all the pressure has released, carefully unlock and remove the lid. Let cool for a few minutes.

6. Meanwhile, in a small bowl, stir together the miso and an equal amount of cool water to dissolve, then add it to the pot and stir through. Taste and season with salt and pepper

---

Ingredient tip: If you don't have miso, use 1 to 2 tablespoons of tamari or soy sauce instead.

PER SERVING Calories: 219; Total fat: 3g; Protein: 14g; Sodium: 269mg; Fiber: 6g

Cheesy Macaroni

PAGE 59

CHAPTER 5

Pasta Perfection

Pasta dishes are such satisfying and comforting meals—and there are so many options for vegans! While using an electric pressure cooker to cook pasta may not save much in terms of total cooking time, it does cook your pasta to a perfect al dente texture without requiring you to stand at the stove. Smaller, rounder shapes work best in the pressure cooker, such as penne, shells, and rotini. All the recipes here can be made with whole-wheat or other whole-grain pasta for maximum nutrition. Just be aware that if you use rice- or corn-based pastas or other gluten-free options, they may come out a bit stickier than pastas containing gluten.

Spice It Up!

Many of these pasta dishes use a tomato sauce because it's so flavorful and cooks beautifully in the pot under pressure. But if you want a simple seasoning after cooking pasta on its own, try adding 1 to 2 teaspoons olive oil, 1 to 2 teaspoons nutritional yeast, and a pinch of grated lemon zest per portion.

It's All about Timing

While exact cooking times are given in these recipes, it really depends on the size and type of pasta you buy. As a general rule, when you look at the cooking time on the package, divide it by two, then subtract 1 to 2 minutes, depending on how soft you like your pasta. A general guideline for the amount of liquid is to use 1 cup water per each 4 ounces of pasta.

Lemon and Olive Pasta

This simple pasta dish has a beautiful blend of flavors. Pair it with a fresh green salad or some greens sautéed with garlic for a complete, satisfying meal. ***Serves 4 to 5***

BUDGET-FRIENDLY, NUT-FREE, SOY-FREE

Prep time: 5 minutes · Cooking setting: Sauté, 7 to 8 minutes, then High Pressure, 4 minutes
Release: Quick · Total time: 25 minutes

- ★ 1 Vidalia onion, diced
- ★ 2 garlic cloves, minced
  1 tablespoon olive oil, plus more as needed
  3½ cups water or unsalted vegetable broth
- ★ 10 ounces bow ties, small shells, or other small pasta (about 3¾ cups)
- ★ Grated zest and juice of 1 lemon
- ★ ¼ cup pitted black olives, chopped
  Salt
  Freshly ground black pepper

1. On your electric pressure cooker, select Sauté. Add the onion, garlic, and olive oil. Cook for 7 to 8 minutes, stirring occasionally, until the onion is lightly browned.

2. Add the water and pasta. Cancel Sauté.

3. Close and lock the lid and ensure the pressure valve is sealed, then select High Pressure and set the time for 4 minutes.

4. Once the cook time is complete, quick release the pressure, being careful not to get your fingers or face near the steam release.

5. Once all the pressure has released, carefully unlock and remove the lid. Stir the pasta and drain any excess water. Stir in the lemon zest and juice and the olives. Taste and add more olive oil and season with salt and pepper.

Ingredient tip: For a change of pace, try this recipe with a generous sprinkle of nutritional yeast instead of the lemon zest and juice.

PER SERVING Calories: 414; Total fat: 7g; Protein: 15g; Sodium: 436mg; Fiber: 9g

Cheesy Macaroni

This recipe uses the pot-in-pot method to make an ooey-gooey macaroni with vegan cheese sauce. If you don't have a steamer, you can cook the macaroni on the stove as per the package directions. *Serves 4*

BUDGET-FRIENDLY, NUT-FREE, SOY-FREE

Prep time: 10 minutes · Cooking setting: High Pressure, 5 minutes · Release: Quick · Total time: 25 minutes

---

★ 1 pound macaroni or other small pasta

5½ cups water, divided

½ to 1 teaspoon salt, plus more as needed

★ 2 yellow potatoes or red potatoes, peeled and cut into chunks

★ 2 carrots, scrubbed or peeled and cut into chunks (of similar size to the potatoes)

½ cup nondairy milk

★ ¼ cup nutritional yeast

★ 1 tablespoon freshly squeezed lemon juice

2 teaspoons onion powder

1 teaspoon garlic powder

Pinch red pepper flakes or cayenne (optional)

1. In your electric pressure cooker's cooking pot, combine the macaroni, 4 cups of water, and a pinch of salt.

2. Place a trivet in the pot and put the potatoes and carrots in a steaming basket on top of the trivet. Close and lock the lid and ensure the pressure valve is sealed, then select High Pressure and set the time for 5 minutes.

3. Once the cook time is complete, quick release the pressure, being careful not to get your fingers or face near the steam release.

4. Once all the pressure has released, remove the lid and carefully pull out the steaming basket with the potatoes and carrots. Transfer to a blender and add the milk, remaining 1½ cups of water, salt, nutritional yeast, lemon juice, onion powder, garlic powder, and red pepper flakes (if using). Purée until smooth. Stir the cheese sauce into the macaroni. Taste and season with more salt or other seasonings, if needed.

Ingredient tip: To get the texture of gooey cheese, use a waxy potato, such as red, yellow, or Yukon Gold instead of a starchy russet or baking potato.

PER SERVING Calories: 501; Total fat: 3g; Protein: 23g; Sodium: 346mg; Fiber: 14g

Creamy Mushroom Rigatoni

Mushrooms add texture and a savory boost to this creamy vegan sauce. *Serves 4*

BUDGET-FRIENDLY, NUT-FREE, SOY-FREE

Prep time: 10 minutes · Cooking setting: Sauté, 7 to 8 minutes, then High Pressure, 3 minutes
Release: Natural for 5 minutes, then Quick · Total time: 35 minutes

---

✸ 12 ounce mushrooms, sliced
(about 5 cups)

2 to 3 teaspoons olive oil

3 cups water or unsalted
vegetable broth

¼ to ½ teaspoon salt, plus
more as needed

✸ 12 ounces rigatoni (about
4½ cups)

✸ 1 cup unsweetened
nondairy milk

✸ 2 tablespoons nutritional yeast

1 tablespoon dried oregano

1 teaspoon onion powder

½ teaspoon garlic powder

¼ teaspoon ground nutmeg
(optional)

Freshly ground black pepper

1. On your electric pressure cooker, select Sauté. Add the mushrooms and olive oil and cook for 7 to 8 minutes, stirring occasionally, until the mushrooms are lightly browned. Cancel Sauté.

2. Add the water, salt, and pasta. Close and lock the lid and ensure the pressure valve is sealed, then select High Pressure and set the time for 3 minutes.

3. Once the cook time is complete, let the pressure release naturally for 5 minutes, then quick release any remaining pressure, being careful not to get your fingers or face near the steam release.

4. Once all the pressure has released, carefully unlock and remove the lid. Drain off any excess water and stir in the milk, nutritional yeast, oregano, onion powder, garlic powder, and nutmeg (if using). Taste and season with more salt, if needed, and pepper. You may have to pull apart any noodles that have stuck together.

5. On the pressure cooker, select Sauté or Simmer. Cook, stirring, for 2 to 3 minutes until the sauce thickens slightly.

Ingredient tip: Oat, cashew, or soy milk works best for this, as these options are thicker than almond or rice milk. You could use canned coconut milk, which is thicker, as long as you don't mind that the coconut flavor and slight sweetness will likely come through. If you can find it, an unsweetened nondairy creamer or barista-grade nondairy milk is ideal.

PER SERVING Calories: 506; Total fat: 6g; Protein: 23g; Sodium: 200mg; Fiber: 12g

Southwest Pasta

Bring a spicy, smoky twist to pasta, along with black beans and corn, for a full, balanced meal. After cooking, you can also toss in some chopped bell pepper, avocado, fresh cilantro, and maybe a sprinkle of grated vegan cheese. For the finishing touch, serve with lime wedges for squeezing. *Serves 4*

BUDGET-FRIENDLY, NUT-FREE, SOY-FREE

Prep time: 5 minutes · Cooking setting: Sauté, 5 to 6 minutes, then High Pressure, 4 minutes
Release: Natural for 4 minutes, then Quick · Total time: 25 minutes

---

✱ 1 red onion, diced

1 to 2 teaspoons olive oil

1 to 2 teaspoons ground chipotle pepper

✱ 1 (28-ounce) can crushed tomatoes

✱ 8 ounces rotini, fusilli, or penne

1 cup water or unsalted vegetable broth

✱ 1½ cups fresh or frozen corn

✱ 1½ cups cooked black beans (from ½ cup dried)

Salt

Freshly ground black pepper

1. On your electric pressure cooker, select Sauté. Add the red onion and olive oil and cook for 5 to 6 minutes, stirring occasionally, until the onion is lightly browned. Cancel Sauté.

2. Stir in the chipotle pepper, tomatoes, pasta, and water. Close and lock the lid and ensure the pressure valve is sealed, then select High Pressure and set the time for 4 minutes.

3. Once the cook time is complete, let the pressure release naturally for 4 minutes, then quick release any remaining pressure, being careful not to get your fingers or face near the steam release.

4. Once all the pressure has released, carefully unlock and remove the lid. Stir in the corn and black beans to warm. Taste and season with salt and pepper.

Substitution tip: If you don't have chipotle pepper on hand, use 2 teaspoons chili powder plus 1 teaspoon smoked paprika.

PER SERVING Calories: 366; Total fat: 4; Protein: 17g; Sodium: 176mg; Fiber: 14g

Peanut Noodles

Carrots and broccoli get steamed on top of and then tossed with these saucy noodles. Use thick noodles that have a suggested stovetop cooking time of at least 8 minutes. *Serves 3 to 4*

BUDGET-FRIENDLY

Prep time: 10 minutes · Cooking setting: Low Pressure, 2 minutes · Release: Quick · Total time: 20 minutes

---

★ ½ cup smooth peanut butter

★ ¼ cup tamari or soy sauce

¼ cup rice vinegar or apple cider vinegar

1 to 2 tablespoons toasted sesame oil (optional)

1 teaspoon ground ginger (optional)

Pinch red pepper flakes or cayenne (optional)

2½ cups water, plus more as needed

★ 8 ounces thick udon noodles or soba noodles

★ 4 carrots, scrubbed or peeled and cut into matchsticks

★ ½ head broccoli, cut into 1-inch pieces

1. In a small bowl, stir together the peanut butter, tamari, vinegar, sesame oil (if using), ginger (if using), and red pepper flakes (if using) until smooth and combined.

2. Pour the peanut sauce into your electric pressure cooker's cooking pot. Add the water.

3. Add the noodles to the pot, breaking them into shorter strands if they're too long to lie flat on the bottom and making sure the liquid covers them. Add another ¼ cup of water, if needed. Stir the noodles a bit to make sure they don't stick together.

4. Lay the carrots and then the broccoli on top, or put them in a steaming basket on top of a trivet. Close and lock the lid and ensure the pressure valve is sealed. Select Low Pressure and set the time for 2 minutes.

5. Once the cook time is complete, quick release the pressure, being careful not to get your fingers or face near the steam release.

6. Once all the pressure has released, remove the lid. Toss everything together, breaking up any noodles that may have stuck together, and serve.

Preparation tip: Garnish with chopped fresh cilantro, chopped scallion and red bell pepper, roasted peanuts, and/or fresh lime juice after cooking.

PER SERVING Calories: 467; Total fat: 20g; Protein: 20g; Sodium: 1.5mg; Fiber: 5g

Red Curry Noodles

These incredibly flavorful noodles are infused with curry, coconut, and lime. The sesame oil adds flavor and helps keep the noodles from sticking together after they're cooked. If you like, add a tablespoon or two of unrefined sugar or brown sugar with the other ingredients. These noodles keep well and make a great base for lunch bowls.
Serves 4

BUDGET-FRIENDLY, NUT-FREE

Prep time: 5 minutes · Cooking setting: High Pressure, 1 minute · Release: Quick · Total time: 15 minutes

2 cups water

★ 1 (13.5-ounce) can coconut milk

★ ¼ cup red curry paste

★ 1 tablespoon freshly squeezed lime juice

★ 1 tablespoon tamari or soy sauce

1 to 2 teaspoons toasted sesame oil

★ 8 ounces thick ramen noodles or wide brown rice noodles

1. In your electric pressure cooker's cooking pot, combine the water, coconut milk, curry paste, lime juice, tamari, and sesame oil. Add the noodles, breaking them into shorter strands if they're too long to lie flat on the bottom. Close and lock the lid and ensure the pressure valve is sealed, then select High Pressure and set the time for 1 minute.

2. Once the cook time is complete, quick release the pressure, being careful not to get your fingers or face near the steam release.

3. Once all the pressure has released, remove the lid. Toss everything together, breaking up any noodles that may have stuck together, and serve.

Serving tip: Top these yummy noodles with chopped veggies, and pair with greens sautéed in sesame oil.

PER SERVING Calories: 611; Total fat: 36g; Protein: 6g; Sodium: 473mg; Fiber: 2g

Sun-Dried Tomato Pasta

In this recipe, pasta is infused with onion and sun-dried tomato flavors, then paired with fresh cherry tomatoes and basil for a classic bowl. Sprinkle with a dusting of nutritional yeast, if you like, or scoop it over some chopped fresh spinach. *Serves 4*

BUDGET-FRIENDLY, NUT-FREE, SOY-FREE

Prep time: 10 minutes · Cooking setting: Sauté, 4 to 5 minutes, then High Pressure, 4 minutes
Release: Natural for 5 minutes, then Quick · Total time: 30 minutes

---

★ 1 large Vidalia onion, diced

1 teaspoon olive oil, plus more for finishing

★ 10 ounces (about 3 cups) penne, rotini, or fusilli

★ ¼ cup sun-dried tomatoes, chopped

2 cups water or unsalted vegetable broth

½ teaspoon salt, plus more as needed

★ 2 tablespoons finely chopped fresh basil

★ 1 cup cherry tomatoes, halved or quartered

½ teaspoon garlic powder (optional)

Freshly ground black pepper

1. On your electric pressure cooker, select Sauté. Add the onion and olive oil and cook for 4 to 5 minutes, stirring occasionally, until the onion is softened.

2. Add the pasta, sun-dried tomatoes, water, and a pinch of salt. Cancel Sauté.

3. Close and lock the lid and ensure the pressure valve is sealed, then select High Pressure and set the time for 4 minutes.

4. Once the cook time is complete, let the pressure release naturally for 5 minutes, then quick release any remaining pressure, being careful not to get your fingers or face near the steam release.

5. Once all the pressure has released, carefully unlock and remove the lid. Select Sauté or Simmer. Toss in the basil, cherry tomatoes, garlic powder (if using), and another drizzle of olive oil. Taste and season with more salt, if needed, and pepper.

Ingredient tip: Use dry sun-dried tomatoes for this recipe, not the ones packed in oil in a jar. If you already have the kind in a jar, add them with the fresh tomatoes and basil after the pasta is finished cooking.

PER SERVING Calories: 343; Total fat: 3g; Protein: 14g; Sodium: 300mg; Fiber: 9g

Tomato Cream Pasta

This one-pot electric pressure cooker recipe leaves you with perfectly cooked pasta in a rich tomato sauce. If you prefer just tomato, omit the nondairy milk or cream and add ½ cup tomato paste with the crushed tomatoes for a richer flavor. *Serves 4*

BUDGET-FRIENDLY, NUT-FREE, SOY-FREE

Prep time: 5 minutes

Cooking setting: High Pressure, 4 minutes, then Sauté or Simmer, 4 to 5 minutes

Release: Natural for 5 minutes, then Quick · Total time: 25 minutes

---

- ⭐ 1 (28-ounce) can crushed tomatoes
- 1 tablespoon dried basil
- ½ teaspoon garlic powder
- ⭐ 10 ounces penne, rotini, or fusilli (about 3 cups)
- ½ teaspoon salt, plus more as needed
- 1½ cups water or unsalted vegetable broth
- ⭐ 1 cup unsweetened nondairy milk or creamer
- ⭐ 2 cups chopped fresh spinach (optional)
- Freshly ground black pepper

1. In your electric pressure cooker's cooking pot, combine the tomatoes, basil, garlic powder, pasta, salt, and water. Close and lock the lid and ensure the pressure valve is sealed, then select High Pressure and set the time for 4 minutes.

2. Once the cook time is complete, let the pressure release naturally for 5 minutes, then quick release any remaining pressure, being careful not to get your fingers or face near the steam release.

3. Once all the pressure has released, carefully unlock and remove the lid. Stir in the milk and spinach (if using). Taste and season with more salt, if needed, and pepper.

4. On your pressure cooker, select Sauté or Simmer. Let cook for 4 to 5 minutes, until the sauce thickens and the greens wilt.

Preparation tip: While vodka cream sauce is always delicious, it's not safe to make in a pressure cooker, as the alcohol level is high enough that it could ignite.

PER SERVING Calories: 321; Total fat: 3g; Protein: 14g; Sodium: 365mg; Fiber: 9g

Penne Arrabbiata

Arrabbiata means "angry" in Italian, and this fiery dish is true to its name! Side benefit of spicy foods: They act as an appetite suppressant to help you avoid overeating this delicious pasta. ***Serves 4***

BUDGET-FRIENDLY, NUT-FREE, SOY-FREE

Prep time: 10 minutes · Cooking setting: Sauté, 4 to 5 minutes, then High Pressure, 4 minutes
Release: Natural for 5 minutes, then Quick · Total time: 30 minutes

---

★ 1 red onion, diced

★ 2 garlic cloves, minced

   1 teaspoon olive oil

★ 1 (28-ounce) can crushed tomatoes

   1½ cups water

★ 10 ounces penne pasta (about 3 cups)

   ½ to 1 teaspoon red pepper flakes

   ½ teaspoon salt, plus more as needed

   Freshly ground black pepper

1. On your electric pressure cooker, select Sauté. Add the red onion, garlic, and olive oil. Cook for 4 to 5 minutes, stirring occasionally, until the onion is softened.

2. Add the tomatoes, water, pasta, red pepper flakes, and salt. Cancel Sauté.

3. Close and lock the lid and ensure the pressure valve is sealed, then select High Pressure and set the time for 4 minutes.

4. Once the cook time is complete, let the pressure release naturally for 5 minutes, then quick release any remaining pressure, being careful not to get your fingers or face near the steam release.

5. Once all the pressure has released, carefully unlock and remove the lid. Taste and season with more salt, if needed, and black pepper.

Ingredient tip: Start small with the spice level. You can always add more after cooking if you need to bump it up, but you can't take it out after it's in there.

PER SERVING Calories: 327; Total fat: 3g; Protein: 14g; Sodium: 317mg; Fiber: 9g

Hummus Noodle Casserole

This recipe might sound weird, but the flavors of hummus go great with pasta, and when you thin hummus out with liquid, it makes a tasty sauce or dressing. This casserole was inspired by the noodle casseroles my mom used to make on really busy weeknights. The peas add a surprising amount of protein, as well as selenium.

Serves 4

BUDGET-FRIENDLY, NUT-FREE, SOY-FREE

Prep time: 5 minutes · Cooking setting: High Pressure, 4 minutes
Release: Natural for 5 minutes, then Quick · Total time: 20 minutes

---

- ★ 1 cup hummus
  3¼ to 3½ cups water and/or unsalted vegetable broth
- ★ 10 ounces penne, bow tie, or small shell pasta (about 3 cups)
- ★ 3 or 4 celery stalks, chopped
  ½ teaspoon sweet paprika
  ½ teaspoon dried thyme
- ★ 1 cup peas
- ★ ¼ to ½ cup fresh parsley, finely chopped
  Salt
  Freshly ground black pepper

1. In your electric pressure cooker's cooking pot, stir together the hummus and water until mostly combined. Add the pasta, celery, paprika, and thyme. If you like your peas fully cooked, add them here, as well as the parsley if you want it to merge into the sauce. Close and lock the lid and ensure the pressure valve is sealed, then select High Pressure and set the time for 4 minutes.

2. Once the cook time is complete, let the pressure release naturally for 5 minutes, then quick release any remaining pressure, being careful not to get your fingers or face near the steam release.

3. Once all the pressure has released, carefully unlock and remove the lid. Stir in the peas and parsley (if you didn't add them in step 1). Taste and season with salt and pepper.

Ingredient tip: Use a mild-flavored hummus for this dish, like plain, garlic, or pine nut. The recipe can work with a roasted red pepper or olive hummus, but the dish will take on a different personality.

PER SERVING Calories: 434; Total fat: 10g; Protein: 16g; Sodium: 30mg; Fiber: 11g

Beet Marinara Sauce

PAGE 79

CHAPTER 6

For the Love of Veggies

A pressure cooker is a great way to make comforting potato, sweet potato, squash, beet, carrot, and parsnip dishes, which pair well with beans and grains to make a relatively light meal—perfect for late-night dinners.

Spice It Up!

Vegetables have a lot more flavor than grains or beans but can benefit from a bit of salt and savory seasoning to offset any inherent bitterness. Some seasonings that add a satisfying dimension to a vegetable dish are olive oil, vegetable broth, vegan margarine, toasted sesame oil, tamari or soy sauce, miso, nutritional yeast, and onion or garlic powder. Because we need to cook with liquid in the pressure cooker, it can dilute the flavors of fresh onion or garlic, so using them in powdered form is a great way to replace that umami depth. If you like a little kick to your food, add a pinch of cayenne or red pepper flakes. Or, for a smoky flavor, add ¼ teaspoon smoked paprika.

Easy on Your Wallet

While fresh, organic vegetables are always the best options, they can be expensive, and if you're cooking for one, you might not get through them before they go bad. Frozen vegetables are a great choice because they're flash frozen and so retain a lot of their nutrients. They help keep costs down and ensure you always have some vegetable on hand to throw into dinner. Some of the best choices to grab from the freezer are peas, corn, broccoli, cauliflower, kale, spinach, green beans, squash, and sweet potatoes.

Mashed Potatoes

Sometimes you just need classic comfort food, and these mashed potatoes can be made easily and quickly in the pressure cooker. Enjoy them as is or dress them up with vegan sour cream and chopped chives. *Serves 4 to 6*

BUDGET-FRIENDLY, GLUTEN-FREE, NUT-FREE, SOY-FREE

Prep time: 10 minutes · Cooking setting: High Pressure, 5 minutes · Release: Quick · Total time: 20 minutes

---

★ 4 to 6 medium russet potatoes, scrubbed or peeled and uniformly chopped (about 5 cups)

★ 1 cup unsalted vegetable broth or water

Salt

★ 2 to 4 tablespoons olive oil, coconut oil, or vegan margarine

★ 2 to 4 tablespoons unsweetened nondairy milk

½ teaspoon garlic powder (optional)

1. In your electric pressure cooker's cooking pot, combine the potatoes, vegetable broth, and a pinch of salt. Close and lock the lid and ensure the pressure valve is sealed, then select High Pressure and set the time for 5 minutes.

2. Once the cook time is complete, quick release the pressure, being careful not to get your fingers or face near the steam release.

3. Once all the pressure has released, carefully unlock and remove the lid. Using oven mitts, lift out the pot.

4. Add the olive oil, milk, and garlic powder (if using) to the pot. Using a potato masher, mash the potatoes. Alternatively, use an immersion blender right in the pot to purée the potatoes to the texture you want. Taste and season with more salt, if needed.

Ingredient tip: Using vegetable broth to cook the potatoes adds more flavor, but use water if you prefer.

PER SERVING Calories: 233; Total fat: 7g; Protein: 4g; Sodium: 162mg; Fiber: 4g

Potato Salad

An easy creamy dressing for some perfectly cooked potatoes makes for a delicious vegan option to take to picnics and cookouts. *Serves 4 to 6*

BUDGET-FRIENDLY, GLUTEN-FREE, NUT-FREE, SOY-FREE

Prep time: 10 minutes · Cooking setting: High Pressure, 6 minutes · Release: Natural · Total time: 30 minutes

- ★ 4 to 6 medium russet potatoes, scrubbed and cut in large uniform cubes (4 to 5 cups)
- ★ ½ cup unsweetened nondairy yogurt
- ★ 2 teaspoons Dijon mustard
  1½ teaspoons apple cider vinegar
  ½ teaspoon onion powder (optional)
  ¼ teaspoon salt
- ★ 3 or 4 celery stalks, chopped
- ★ 2 scallions, chopped
  Freshly ground black pepper

1. Put the potatoes in a steaming basket.

2. Put a trivet in your electric pressure cooker's cooking pot, pour in a cup or two of water, and set the steaming basket on the trivet. (Alternatively, you can cook the potatoes right in the water, though they will end up quite a bit softer.) Close and lock the lid and ensure the pressure valve is sealed, then select High Pressure and set the time for 6 minutes.

3. Once the cook time is complete, let the pressure release naturally, about 10 minutes.

4. Meanwhile, in a large bowl, stir together the yogurt, mustard, vinegar, onion powder (if using), and salt. Add the celery and scallions and stir to combine.

5. Once all the pressure has released, carefully unlock and remove the lid. Using oven mitts, carefully lift the steaming basket out of the pot (or drain the potatoes if you cooked them directly in the water). Let the potatoes cool for a few minutes, then stir them into the bowl with the vegetables and dressing. Taste and season with pepper.

Variation tip: Add a large handful of chopped fresh parsley and/or spinach to boost the nutritional content of your salad.

PER SERVING Calories: 201; Total fat: 1g; Protein: 5g; Sodium: 52mg; Fiber: 5g

Spicy Potato Bites with Avocado Dip

Try this recipe the next time you need an excellent brunch dish or something to serve with roasted portobello mushrooms. *Serves 4*

BUDGET-FRIENDLY, GLUTEN-FREE, NUT-FREE, SOY-FREE

Prep time: 10 minutes · Cooking setting: High Pressure, 6 minutes, then Sauté, 2 minutes
Release: Natural · Total time: 30 minutes

★ 4 to 6 medium russet potatoes, scrubbed and cut in large uniform cubes (4 to 5 cups)

★ 1 avocado, peeled and pitted

★ 2 tablespoons freshly squeezed lime juice

2 teaspoons onion powder, divided

1 teaspoon garlic powder, divided

Pinch salt

1 to 2 tablespoons water, if needed

1 tablespoon olive oil

½ teaspoon smoked paprika

¼ teaspoon ground chipotle pepper

1. Put the potatoes in a steaming basket.

2. Put a trivet in your electric pressure cooker's cooking pot, pour in a cup or two of water, and set the steaming basket on top. Close and lock the lid and ensure the pressure valve is sealed. Select High Pressure and set the time for 6 minutes.

3. Once the cook time is complete, let the pressure release naturally, about 10 minutes.

4. In a blender, combine the avocado, lime juice, 1 teaspoon of onion powder, ½ teaspoon of garlic powder, and the salt. Purée, adding the water if needed to achieve your preferred consistency. Transfer to a serving bowl.

5. Once all the pressure has released, carefully unlock and remove the lid. Using oven mitts, lift the steaming basket out of the pot.

6. Put the empty pot back into the pressure cooker and select Sauté. Return the potatoes to the pot and add the olive oil, remaining 1 teaspoon of onion powder, remaining ½ teaspoon of garlic powder, paprika, and chipotle pepper. Cook for about 2 minutes, stirring occasionally, until any liquid has evaporated. Serve the potatoes with the avocado dipping sauce.

PER SERVING Calories: 205; Total fat: 6g; Protein: 4g; Sodium: 153mg; Fiber: 5g

Lemon-Dill Baby Potatoes

Pairing baby potatoes with fresh, zingy lemon and dill produces the ultimate spring-time vibe. Make these as a side for your next veggie burger night. *Serves 4*

BUDGET-FRIENDLY, GLUTEN-FREE, NUT-FREE, SOY-FREE

Prep time: 5 minutes · Cooking setting: High Pressure, 10 minutes · Release: Natural · Total time: 25 minutes

⭐ 2 pounds baby potatoes, scrubbed

2 tablespoons olive oil

⭐ 2 tablespoons freshly squeezed lemon juice

⭐ 1 teaspoon dried dill

⭐ 2 tablespoons nutritional yeast (optional)

Salt

1. Pour a cup or two of water into your electric pressure cooker's cooking pot and add the potatoes. Close and lock the lid and ensure the pressure valve is sealed, then select High Pressure and set the time for 10 minutes.

2. Once the cook time is complete, let the pressure release naturally, about 10 minutes.

3. Once all the pressure has released, carefully unlock and remove the lid. Drain the potatoes.

4. In a small bowl, whisk together the olive oil, lemon juice, dill, and nutritional yeast (if using). Add to the pot and toss the potatoes to coat.

Preparation tip: If you want to infuse more flavor into your potatoes, pour the water in the pot, toss the potatoes in a large bowl with the dressing, and steam them in a dish above the water.

PER SERVING Calories: 218; Total fat: 7g; Protein: 6g; Sodium: 80mg; Fiber: 4g

Sweet Potato Breakfast Bowls

When you get sick of porridge, toast, or cereal, try sweet potatoes for breakfast! The apple or pear adds a nice bit of sweetness—peel it if you like, or leave the peel on for new nutrients and fiber. This recipe makes two servings, but you can easily double or triple it to make more for the week. *Serves 2*

BUDGET-FRIENDLY, GLUTEN-FREE, SOY-FREE

Prep time: 10 minutes · Cooking setting: High Pressure, 6 minutes · Release: Natural · Total time: 30 minutes

---

★ 1 sweet potato, peeled and chopped

★ 1 apple or pear, cored and quartered

★ ½ cup nondairy milk, plus more as needed

★ 2 tablespoons nut or seed butter (almond, cashew, sunflower)

¼ teaspoon ground cinnamon (optional)

Pinch ground nutmeg (optional)

★ Unrefined sugar or pure maple syrup, for serving (optional)

1. In a heat-proof dish that fits inside your electric pressure cooker's cooking pot, combine the sweet potato and apple.

2. Put a trivet in the pot, pour in a cup or two of water, and set the dish on the trivet. If it's a tight fit, use a foil sling or silicone helper handles to lower the dish onto the trivet (see page 5). Close and lock the lid and ensure the pressure valve is sealed, then select High Pressure and set the time for 6 minutes.

3. Once the cook time is complete, let the pressure release naturally, about 10 minutes.

4. Once all the pressure has released, carefully unlock and remove the lid. Let cool for a few minutes before carefully lifting out the dish with oven mitts or tongs. Transfer the sweet potatoes and apples to a blender.

5. Add the milk, nut butter, cinnamon (if using), and nutmeg (if using). Purée. Add more milk if needed, plus sugar or maple syrup, if you like.

Serving tip: Top with something crunchy, such as chopped fresh apples, slivered almonds, pumpkin seeds, or granola.

PER SERVING Calories: 302; Total fat: 13g; Protein: 6g; Sodium: 115mg; Fiber: 8g

Balsamic and Red Wine Mushrooms

This is an incredibly easy dish, but the flavor is off the charts. It's especially nice served over cooked whole grains or mashed potatoes to soak up any extra sauce.
Serves 4

BUDGET-FRIENDLY, GLUTEN-FREE, NUT-FREE, SOY-FREE

Prep time: 5 minutes · Cooking setting: High Pressure, 2 minutes · Release: Quick · Total time: 15 minutes

---

★ ¼ cup dry red wine

¼ cup water

2 tablespoons balsamic vinegar

1 tablespoon olive oil

★ 1 teaspoon cornstarch or arrowroot powder

½ teaspoon dried basil or mixed herbs

¼ teaspoon salt, plus more as needed

Freshly ground black pepper

★ 1 pound white mushrooms, quartered

1. In your electric pressure cooker's cooking pot, stir together the red wine, water, vinegar, olive oil, cornstarch, basil, and salt. Season with pepper. Add the mushrooms to the sauce. Close and lock the lid and ensure the pressure valve is sealed, then select High Pressure and set the time for 2 minutes.

2. Once the cook time is complete, quick release the pressure, being careful not to get your fingers or face near the steam release.

3. Once all the pressure has released, carefully unlock and remove the lid. Taste and season with more salt and pepper, if needed.

PER SERVING Calories: 72; Total fat: 3g; Protein: 2g; Sodium: 151mg; Fiber: 0g

Ratatouille

Ratatouille tastes best with the freshest produce, so scout your local farmers' market to get these beautiful veggies when they're in season. *Serves 4 to 6*

BUDGET-FRIENDLY, GLUTEN-FREE, NUT-FREE, SOY-FREE

Prep time: 10 minutes · Cooking setting: Sauté, 4 to 5 minutes, then High Pressure, 6 minutes
Release: Natural · Total time: 45 minutes

☆ 1 onion, diced

☆ 4 garlic cloves, minced

1 to 2 teaspoons olive oil

1 cup water

☆ 3 or 4 tomatoes, diced

☆ 1 eggplant, cubed

☆ 1 or 2 bell peppers, any color, seeded and chopped

1½ tablespoons dried herbes de Provence (or any mixture of dried basil, oregano, thyme, marjoram, and rosemary)

½ teaspoon salt

Freshly ground black pepper

1. On your electric pressure cooker, select Sauté. Add the onion, garlic, and olive oil. Cook for 4 to 5 minutes, stirring occasionally, until the onion is softened. Add the water, tomatoes, eggplant, bell peppers, and herbes de Provence. Cancel Sauté.

2. Close and lock the lid and ensure the pressure valve is sealed, then select High Pressure and set the time for 6 minutes.

3. Once the cook time is complete, let the pressure release naturally, about 20 minutes.

4. Once all the pressure has released, carefully unlock and remove the lid. Let cool for a few minutes, then season with salt and pepper.

Serving tip: Serve with couscous or rice, and maybe a sprinkle of toasted pine nuts on top!

PER SERVING Calories: 101; Total fat: 2g; Protein: 4g; Sodium: 304mg; Fiber: 7g

Spaghetti Squash Primavera

Did you know you can cook a whole spaghetti squash without having to cut it open? Spaghetti squash is a great low-carb alternative for pasta, and you can pair it with any sauce—but this simple primavera is an especially tasty option. *Serves 3 to 4*

GLUTEN-FREE, NUT-FREE, SOY-FREE

Prep time: 5 minutes · Cooking setting: High Pressure, 10 to 15 minutes · Release: Natural · Total time: 35 minutes

---

- ★ 1 spaghetti squash
- ★ 2 or 3 garlic cloves, minced
- 1 to 2 tablespoons olive oil or vegan margarine, plus more as needed
- ★ 1 cup peas
- ★ 2 to 3 tablespoons nutritional yeast, plus more as needed
- Salt
- ★ 1 cup cherry tomatoes, halved
- Freshly ground black pepper

1. Put the spaghetti squash in your electric pressure cooker's cooking pot. (If the squash won't fit, cut it in half, scoop out the seeds with a large spoon, and stack the halves in the pot cut-side down.) Pour in a cup or two of water. Close and lock the lid and ensure the pressure valve is sealed, then select High Pressure and set the time for 10 to 15 minutes, depending on the size of your squash. (If you've cut the squash in half, set the time for 5 to 7 minutes, depending on size.)

2. Once the cook time is complete, let the pressure release naturally, about 10 minutes.

3. Once all the pressure has released, carefully unlock and remove the lid. Using tongs or a large fork and spoon, carefully lift out the squash and set it aside to cool.

4. Empty the water from the pot and return the pot to the pressure cooker. Select Sauté. Add the garlic and olive oil and cook for about 2 minutes, stirring occasionally, until the garlic is lightly browned. Add the peas and cook for 1 to 2 minutes to soften. ➤

5. If the squash is whole, cut it in half and scoop out the seeds. Using a fork, scrape the squash flesh into strands and return them to the pot. Sprinkle the strands with the nutritional yeast and season with salt. Toss to coat in the oil.

6. Add the cherry tomatoes, plus more nutritional yeast, olive oil, salt, and pepper, if needed.

Variation tip: To make a delicious and protein-rich topping for this dish, pulse together some cooked chickpeas and pitted black olives in a food processor until finely chopped.

PER SERVING Calories: 165; Total fat: 6g; Protein: 8g; Sodium: 126mg; Fiber: 5g

Beet Marinara Sauce

For those allergic or sensitive to tomatoes, here's a recipe for a tomato-free red sauce for pasta. It's full of nutrient-dense carrots and beets instead, so you can get your fill of vitamin C and folate. *Serves 6*

BUDGET-FRIENDLY, GLUTEN-FREE, NUT-FREE, SOY-FREE

Prep time: 10 minutes · Cooking setting: Sauté, 2 to 3 minutes, then High Pressure, 10 minutes

Release: Natural · Total time: 45 minutes

★ 1 onion, diced

★ 2 garlic cloves, minced

  1 tablespoon olive oil

★ 6 to 8 carrots, peeled or scrubbed and chopped (about 5 cups)

★ 2 medium beets, scrubbed and chopped (about 2 cups)

  1 teaspoon salt, plus more as needed

  1 cup water

  1 tablespoon dried basil

★ 2 tablespoons freshly squeezed lemon juice

  Freshly ground black pepper

1. On your electric pressure cooker, select Sauté. Add the onion, garlic, and olive oil. Cook for 2 to 3 minutes, stirring occasionally, until the onion is softened. Add the carrots, beets, salt, and water. Cancel Sauté.

2. Close and lock the lid and ensure the pressure valve is sealed, then select High Pressure and set the time for 10 minutes.

3. Once the cook time is complete, let the pressure release naturally, about 15 minutes.

4. Once all the pressure has released, carefully unlock and remove the lid. Stir in the basil and lemon juice. Let cool for a few minutes, then purée the beets and carrots—either use an immersion blender right in the pot or transfer to a countertop blender and add more water, if needed. Taste and season with more salt and pepper, if needed.

Ingredient tip: If you have fresh basil, use a small handful instead of the dried for a fresh boost of flavor.

PER SERVING Calories: 97; Total fat: 3g; Protein: 2g; Sodium: 498mg; Fiber: 5g

Butternut Squash and Pineapple

Pineapple adds the digestion-aiding enzyme bromelain to this recipe. *Serves 4*

BUDGET-FRIENDLY, NUT-FREE

Prep time: 5 minutes · Cooking setting: High Pressure, 10 to 15 minutes, then Sauté, 4 to 5 minutes
Release: Natural · Total time: 35 minutes

★ 1 butternut squash

★ 4 cups chopped bok choy

★ 1 scallion, chopped

   1 to 2 teaspoons toasted sesame oil

★ 10 ounces bite-size pineapple chunks (about 1½ cups)

★ 1 to 2 tablespoons tamari or soy sauce

1. Put the butternut squash in your electric pressure cooker's cooking pot. (If the squash won't fit, cut it in half lengthwise, scoop out the seeds with a large spoon, and stack the halves in the pot, cut-side down.) Pour in a cup or two of water. Close and lock the lid and ensure the pressure valve is sealed, then select High Pressure and set the time for 10 to 15 minutes, depending on the size of your squash. (If you've cut the squash in half, set the time for 5 to 7 minutes, depending on size.)

2. Once the cook time is complete, let the pressure release naturally, about 10 minutes.

3. Once all the pressure has released, carefully unlock and remove the lid. Using tongs or a large fork and spoon, carefully lift the squash out of the pot and let cool for a few minutes.

4. Empty the water from the pot and return the pot to the pressure cooker. Select Sauté. Add the bok choy, scallion, and sesame oil. Cook for 1 minute, stirring occasionally, until the vegetables are softened.

5. If the squash is whole, cut it in half lengthwise, scoop out the seeds, and remove the skin. Chop the squash into bite-size chunks and add them to the pot, along with the pineapple and tamari. Toss to combine until heated through.

PER SERVING Calories: 193; Total fat: 8g; Protein: 6g; Sodium: 259mg; Fiber: 5g

Green Pea and Cauliflower Curry

Here's a light dish to have on those nights when you want to get your fill of nutrients but not feel too full. Peas contain lots of protein, zinc, and carotenoids that help keep our eyes healthy. Cauliflower and peas cook relatively quickly, so this recipe is cooked on low pressure. Serve it over brown rice or couscous. *Serves 4*

BUDGET-FRIENDLY, GLUTEN-FREE, NUT-FREE, SOY-FREE

Prep time: 5 minutes · Cooking setting: Low Pressure, 1 to 2 minutes · Release: Quick · Total time: 17 minutes

★ 1 (1-inch) piece fresh ginger, peeled and minced (optional)

1 tablespoon coconut oil or olive oil

★ 1 head cauliflower, chopped

★ 1 (28-ounce) can crushed tomatoes

★ 2 cups frozen peas

1 cup water

★ 2 tablespoons tomato paste

1 tablespoon curry powder

Salt

Freshly ground black pepper

1. On your electric pressure cooker, select Sauté. Add the ginger (if using) and coconut oil and cook for 2 to 3 minutes, stirring occasionally, until the ginger is softened.

2. Add the cauliflower, tomatoes, peas, water, tomato paste, and curry powder and stir to combine. Cancel Sauté.

3. Close and lock the lid and ensure the pressure valve is sealed, then select Low Pressure and set the time for 1 to 2 minutes, depending on how soft you like your cauliflower.

4. Once the cook time is complete, quick release the pressure, being careful not to get your fingers or face near the steam release.

5. Once all the pressure has released, carefully unlock and remove the lid. Taste and season with salt and pepper.

Serving tip: Top with chopped fresh cilantro or fresh mint if you have some on hand.

PER SERVING Calories: 158; Total fat: 5g; Protein: 8g; Sodium: 131mg; Fiber: 9g

Balsamic and Allspice–Pickled Beets

Earthy beets take on a whole different persona when they're cooked with bright vinegar. Keep these in the fridge to add to salads or stir into a basic vegetable soup. *Serves 4 to 8*

BUDGET-FRIENDLY, GLUTEN-FREE, NUT-FREE, SOY-FREE

Prep time: 5 minutes · Cooking setting: High Pressure, 8 minutes · Release: Quick · Total time: 20 minutes

½ cup balsamic vinegar

¼ cup apple cider vinegar

★ 3 tablespoons unrefined sugar

1 teaspoon salt

½ teaspoon ground coriander *or* 1 teaspoon coriander seeds

½ teaspoon ground allspice *or* 1 teaspoon allspice berries

½ cup water

★ 3 or 4 large beets, peeled and sliced

1. In your electric pressure cooker's cooking pot, stir together the vinegars, sugar, salt, coriander, allspice, and water. Add the beets. Close and lock the lid and ensure the pressure valve is sealed, then select High Pressure and set the time for 8 minutes.

2. Once the cook time is complete, quick release the pressure, being careful not to get your fingers or face near the steam release.

3. Once all the pressure has released, carefully unlock and remove the lid. Let cool for a few minutes with the lid off to dissipate the vinegar steam, then scoop out the beets and serve.

Make-ahead tip: If keeping the beets for later, transfer them to an airtight container, ladle in enough liquid to cover them, and refrigerate until needed.

PER SERVING Calories: 102; Total fat: 0g; Protein: 2g; Sodium: 661mg; Fiber: 3g

Spicy, Sweet, and Sour Kale and Kabocha Squash

No Kabocha squash available? Butternut squash makes a good stand-in. *Serves 3 to 4*

BUDGET-FRIENDLY, NUT-FREE

Prep time: 5 minutes · Cooking setting: High Pressure, 10 to 15 minutes, then Sauté, 1 minute

Release: Natural · Total time: 35 minutes

★ 1 kabocha squash

★ 3 or 4 kale leaves, chopped

1 to 2 teaspoons toasted sesame oil

★ ¼ cup tamari or soy sauce

2 tablespoons brown rice vinegar

★ 1 tablespoon pure maple syrup or unrefined sugar

⅛ to ¼ teaspoon red pepper flakes

1. Put the whole squash in your electric pressure cooker's cooking pot. (If the squash won't fit, cut it in half lengthwise, scoop out the seeds with a large spoon, and put the halves in the pot, cut-side down.) Pour in a cup or two of water. Close and lock the lid and ensure the pressure valve is sealed, then select High Pressure and set the time for 10 to 15 minutes, depending on the size of your squash. (If you've cut the squash in half, set the time for 5 to 7 minutes, depending on size.)

2. Once the cook time is complete, let the pressure release naturally, about 10 minutes.

3. Once all the pressure has released, remove the lid. Using tongs or a large fork and spoon, carefully lift the squash out of the pot and let it cool for a few minutes.

4. Empty the water from the pot and return the pot to the pressure cooker. Select Sauté. Add the kale and sesame oil and cook for about 1 minute, stirring occasionally, until the kale is wilted. Add the tamari, vinegar, maple syrup, and red pepper flakes.

5. Halve the squash lengthwise, scoop out the seeds, and remove the skin. Add the squash to the pot, breaking it up in the pot with a wooden spoon. (Alternatively, you can cut the cooked squash into chunks, then add them to the pot.) Stir to combine the squash and seasonings.

PER SERVING Calories: 168; Total fat: 2g; Protein: 7g; Sodium: 1.4g; Fiber: 6g

Miso-Dressed Eggplant

Eggplant will absorb any flavors you cook it with, and here we infuse it with salty, savory miso. You can find miso paste in the refrigerated section of most organic and health food stores. It's a cultured soy product, kind of a relative of soy sauce. Serve the eggplant over cooked quinoa, brown rice, or couscous. *Serves 4*

BUDGET-FRIENDLY, NUT-FREE

Prep time: 5 minutes · Cooking setting: High Pressure, 6 minutes · Release: Natural · Total time: 21 minutes

---

★ ¼ cup white or red miso paste

   3 tablespoons water

★ 1 tablespoon unrefined sugar

★ 1 tablespoon tomato paste

   1 teaspoon toasted sesame oil

★ 1 eggplant, cubed

1. In a large bowl, stir together the miso, water, sugar, tomato paste, and sesame oil until smooth and creamy. Add the eggplant and toss to coat with the dressing. Transfer the eggplant to a heat-proof dish that fits inside your electric pressure cooker's cooking pot.

2. Put a trivet in the pot, pour in a cup or two of water, and set the dish on the trivet. If it's a tight fit, use a foil sling or silicone helper handles to lower the dish onto the trivet (see page 5). Close and lock the lid and ensure the pressure valve is sealed, then select High Pressure and set the time for 6 minutes.

3. Once the cook time is complete, let the pressure release naturally, about 10 minutes.

4. Once all the pressure has released, carefully unlock and remove the lid. Using oven mitts, lift the dish out of the pot and serve.

PER SERVING Calories: 69; Total fat: 2g; Protein: 3g; Sodium: 527mg; Fiber: 4g

Maple-Balsamic Parsnips

Parsnips have a similar texture to carrots, but a distinctive tang that pairs perfectly with balsamic vinegar and maple syrup. *Serves 4*

BUDGET-FRIENDLY, GLUTEN-FREE, NUT-FREE, SOY-FREE

Prep time: 5 minutes · Cooking setting: High Pressure, 6 minutes · Release: Natural · Total time: 21 minutes

---

★ 2 or 3 parsnips, peeled and chopped

★ 1 garlic clove, minced

2 tablespoons balsamic vinegar

★ 1 tablespoon pure maple syrup

1 tablespoon olive oil

½ teaspoon dried thyme leaves *or* ¼ teaspoon ground thyme

Pinch salt

1. In a heat-proof dish that fits inside your electric pressure cooker's cooking pot, combine the parsnips, garlic, vinegar, maple syrup, olive oil, thyme, and salt.

2. Put a trivet in the pot, pour in a cup or two of water, and set the dish on the trivet. If it's a tight fit, use a foil sling or silicone helper handles to lower the dish onto the trivet (see page 5). Close and lock the lid and ensure the pressure valve is sealed, then select High Pressure and set the time for 6 minutes.

3. Once the cook time is complete, let the pressure release naturally, about 10 minutes.

4. Once all the pressure has released, carefully unlock and remove the lid. Using oven mitts, lift out the dish and serve.

PER SERVING Calories: 76; Total fat: 3g; Protein: 1g; Sodium: 62mg; Fiber: 2g

Lavender-Peach Iced Tea

PAGE 88

CHAPTER 7

Holidays and Social Gatherings

Your first thought about using an electric pressure cooker might have to do with the practicality of saving time on beans, whole grains, and soups, but you can also use it to create delicious drinks and appetizers. You might offer to bring these dishes to a party or holiday get-together, especially if you don't know whether there will be many (or any) vegan options. Then you know you'll have something to eat—and it's a fun way to introduce your family and friends to vegan foods at the same time! The pressure cooker is also a great option when you're hosting a party at your house, since you don't have to heat up your kitchen or worry about watching the stove or oven.

Spice It Up!
A few recipes in this chapter call for smoked paprika because the flavor is incomparable. While it's not necessary, a little goes a long way in impressing nonvegan taste buds with its rich smokiness. Nutritional yeast is another seasoning that's worth looking for. Along with onion powder and garlic powder, nutritional yeast brings a savory flavor that pleases the part of our palate that isn't satisfied with just greens and veggies. When cooking for others, it's important to use these kinds of seasonings—along with some oil and salt where it makes sense—to make sure plant foods satisfy an omnivore's taste buds.

Lavender-Peach Iced Tea

Get ready for summer picnics and cookouts with this full-bodied iced tea—without any bitterness from longer steep times. It's easy to make—and also easy to change up the fruit flavor. Try frozen mango, blackberries, raspberries, or any other fruit you enjoy. Keep this thirst-quenching drink on hand to help you stay hydrated, or take it to work in a reusable bottle for an affordable lunch or afternoon drink. Serve with lemon wedges, if you like. ***Makes 8 cups***

BUDGET-FRIENDLY, GLUTEN-FREE, NUT-FREE, SOY-FREE

Prep time: 5 minutes · Cooking setting: High Pressure, 4 minutes · Release: Natural · Total time: 25 minutes

---

* 1 cup chopped fresh or frozen peaches

* 6 black tea bags *or* 2 tablespoons loose black tea in a sealed pouch

* ½ teaspoon dried culinary-grade lavender

* 2 tablespoons freshly squeezed lemon juice

    8 cups water

* 2 to 4 tablespoons unrefined sugar or pure maple syrup (optional)

1. In your electric pressure cooker's cooking pot, combine the peaches, tea, lavender, lemon juice, and water. Close and lock the lid and ensure the pressure valve is sealed, then select High Pressure and set the time for 4 minutes.

2. Once the cook time is complete, let the pressure release naturally, about 15 minutes.

3. Once all the pressure has released, carefully unlock and remove the lid. Stir in the sugar (if using). Let cool before straining and transferring to a pitcher. Keep refrigerated and add ice to serve.

Variation tip: No lavender? No worries. This tea is delicious even without it. Tea time is relaxing time!

PER SERVING (1 cup) Calories: 17; Total fat: 0g; Protein: 0g; Sodium: 0mg; Fiber: 0g

Spinach-Artichoke Dip

Thick and creamy, this dip is perfect for dunking with chunks of pumpernickel bread or thick pita chips. Instead of spinach, you could try other greens—soft red Russian kale is wonderful. If you like your dips on the tangy side, a tablespoon of freshly squeezed lemon juice does the trick, added along with the vinegar. *Makes 2½ cups*

GLUTEN-FREE, SOY-FREE

Prep time: 5 minutes · Cooking setting: High Pressure, 4 minutes · Release: Natural · Total time: 20 minutes

---

★ 1 cup raw cashews

★ 1 cup unsweetened nondairy milk

★ 1 tablespoon nutritional yeast

1½ tablespoons apple cider vinegar

1 teaspoon onion powder

½ teaspoon garlic powder

½ to 1 teaspoon salt

★ 1 (14-ounce) can artichoke hearts in water *or* 1½ cups frozen artichokes, thawed

★ 2 cups fresh spinach

1. In a high-speed blender, combine the cashews, milk, nutritional yeast, vinegar, onion powder, garlic powder, and salt. Purée until smooth and creamy, about 1 minute. Add the artichoke hearts and spinach and pulse a few times to chop up a bit. Pour the mixture into a 7- to 8-inch round baking dish that fits inside your electric pressure cooker.

2. Put a trivet in the pressure cooker's cooking pot, pour in a cup or two of water, and set the baking dish on the trivet. If it's a tight fit, use a foil sling or silicone helper handles to lower the dish onto the trivet (see page 5). Close and lock the lid and ensure the pressure valve is sealed, then select High Pressure and set the time for 4 minutes. ➤

3. Once the cook time is complete, let the pressure release naturally, about 10 minutes.

4. Once all the pressure has released, carefully unlock and remove the lid. Let the baking dish cool for a few minutes before carefully lifting it out of the pot with oven mitts. Serve the dip in the baking dish, or transfer it to a bowl or platter.

Ingredient tip: If you don't have a high-speed blender, soak the cashews in boiling water for a few minutes before blending to get the creamiest consistency. Measure them dry, and fully drain them before putting in the blender.

PER SERVING (½ cup) Calories: 297; Total fat: 21g; Protein: 11g; Sodium: 305mg; Fiber: 5g

Creamy Baba Ghanoush

Instead of roasting eggplant, you can pressure cook it quickly and then add some smokiness with paprika. This baba ghanoush is definitely a creamy dip, perfect to serve with toasted pita wedges, Melba toasts, or crackers that have some texture and crunch.
Makes 2 cups

GLUTEN-FREE, NUT-FREE, SOY-FREE

Prep time: 10 minutes · Cooking setting: High Pressure, 4 minutes · Release: Quick · Total time: 20 minutes

---

* 2 eggplants, peeled and cut into large uniform cubes

  Salt
* ¼ cup tahini
* Juice of 1 lemon

  1 to 2 tablespoons olive oil, plus more as needed

  ¼ teaspoon garlic powder *or* 1 small garlic clove, peeled

  ¼ teaspoon smoked paprika

  Freshly ground black pepper
* 2 tablespoons finely minced fresh mint

1. In a heat-proof dish that fits inside your electric pressure cooker's cooking pot, toss together the eggplant and a pinch of salt.

2. Put a trivet in the pot, pour in a cup or two of water, and set the dish on the trivet. If it's a tight fit, use a foil sling or silicone helper handles to lower the dish onto the trivet (see page 5). Close and lock the lid and ensure the pressure valve is sealed, then select High Pressure and set the time for 4 minutes.

3. Once the cook time is complete, quick release the pressure, being careful not to get your fingers or face near the steam release.

4. Once all the pressure has released, carefully unlock and remove the lid. Carefully lift out the dish with tongs or oven mitts. Transfer the eggplant to a food processor.

5. Add the tahini, lemon juice, olive oil, garlic powder, paprika, and ¼ teaspoon salt. Pulse or purée the mixture until smooth. Taste and season with more salt and pepper, plus a drizzle of olive oil, if needed. Sprinkle the mint on top, or stir it through if you prefer.

PER SERVING (¼ cup) Calories: 71; Total fat: 6g; Protein: 2g; Sodium: 82mg; Fiber: 2g

Brilliant Beet Hummus

Give regular hummus a boost of nutrition, flavor, and color by blending in some beets! Beets have their own phytonutrient, called betalain, which has antioxidant, anti-inflammatory, and detox powers. Betalains degrade with longer cooking times, so cooking beets quickly in the pressure cooker is the best way to go! *Makes 3 cups*

BUDGET-FRIENDLY, GLUTEN-FREE, NUT-FREE, SOY-FREE

Prep time: 10 minutes (to cook the chickpeas) · Cooking setting: High Pressure, 33 minutes
Release: Natural · Total time: 1 hour, 25 minutes

- ★ 1 cup dried chickpeas
  5 cups water, divided, plus more as needed
- ★ 2 large or 3 medium beets, peeled and quartered
- ★ ¼ cup tahini
- ★ Grated zest and juice of 1 lime
- ★ 1 or 2 garlic cloves, peeled
  ¼ to ½ teaspoon salt
  Olive oil, for blending (optional)

1. In your electric pressure cooker's cooking pot, combine the chickpeas and 4 cups of water. Close and lock the lid and ensure the pressure valve is sealed, then select High Pressure and set the time for 25 minutes.

2. Once the cook time is complete, let the pressure release naturally, about 30 minutes.

3. Once all the pressure has released, carefully unlock and remove the lid. Drain and rinse the chickpeas, drain again, and put them back in the pot.

4. Add the beets and remaining 1 cup of water. Close and lock the lid and ensure the pressure valve is sealed, then select High Pressure and set the time for 8 minutes.

5. Once the cook time is complete, let the pressure release naturally, about 10 minutes.

6. Once all the pressure has released, carefully unlock and remove the lid. Drain off any excess water and transfer the chickpeas and beets to a food processor.

7. Add the tahini, lime zest and juice, garlic, and salt. Purée until creamy. The beets should have enough moisture to get a creamy consistency, but you may want to add a tablespoon or two of water and/or olive oil to get the consistency you like in your hummus.

Substitution tip: While the brilliant red-purple of beets makes for a spectacular-looking hummus, you can also make this recipe with pumpkin, winter squash, or carrots.

PER SERVING (¼ cup) Calories: 109; Total fat: 4g; Protein: 5g; Sodium: 75mg; Fiber: 4g

Jalapeño, Carrot, and White Bean Dip

This zesty, flavorful bean dip really jazzes things up. The key to achieving a smooth and creamy consistency is to cook the carrots, which happens so much faster in the pressure cooker than on the stovetop. *Makes 3 cups*

BUDGET-FRIENDLY, GLUTEN-FREE, NUT-FREE, SOY-FREE

Prep time: 10 minutes · Cooking setting: High Pressure, 3 minutes · Release: Quick · Total time: 20 minutes

---

* 2 cups cooked white beans (from ¾ cup dried)
* 4 or 5 carrots, scrubbed or peeled and chopped (about 2 cups)

  1 cup water
* 1 or 2 jalapeño peppers, seeded and chopped
* 2 tablespoons tahini
* Grated zest and juice of 1 lime

  1 teaspoon regular or smoked paprika

  1 to 2 tablespoons olive oil or water (optional)

  ½ to ¾ teaspoon salt

  Freshly ground black pepper

1. In your electric pressure cooker's cooking pot, combine the white beans, carrots, and water. Close and lock the lid and ensure the pressure valve is sealed, then select High Pressure and set the time for 3 minutes.

2. Once the cook time is complete, quick release the pressure, being careful not to get your fingers or face near the steam release.

3. Once all the pressure has released, carefully unlock and remove the lid. Drain any excess water and transfer the beans and carrots to a food processor or small blender.

4. Add the jalapeños, tahini, lime zest and juice, and paprika. Purée, adding the olive oil, 1 tablespoon at a time, to achieve the desired texture. Taste and season with the salt and pepper.

Variation tip: Try sweet potato or winter squash instead of carrots for a different flavor.

PER SERVING (¼ cup) Calories: 74; Total fat: 3g; Protein: 3g; Sodium: 115mg; Fiber: 3g

White Bean Crostini

Crostini are toasted breads with a savory topping. Here, they are topped with a protein-rich white bean tapenade. The tapenade also makes a lovely filling for wraps or lettuce cups. *Serves 12*

BUDGET-FRIENDLY, NUT-FREE, SOY-FREE

Prep time: 10 minutes · Cooking setting: High Pressure, 30 minutes · Release: Natural · Total time: 55 minutes

- ⭐ 1 cup dried white beans
- 2 cups water or unsalted vegetable broth
- ⭐ ⅓ cup pitted black olives or green olives, chopped, plus more for topping
- ⭐ ¼ red onion, finely diced
- ⭐ 2 tablespoons finely chopped fresh mint or parsley
- 1 tablespoon olive oil (optional)
- Salt
- Freshly ground black pepper
- ⭐ 1 baguette, sliced and toasted

1. In your electric pressure cooker's cooking pot, combine the white beans and water. Close and lock the lid and ensure the pressure valve is sealed, then select High Pressure and set the time for 30 minutes.

2. Once the cook time is complete, let the pressure release naturally, about 15 minutes.

3. Once all the pressure has released, carefully unlock and remove the lid. Stir in the olives, red onion, mint, and olive oil (if using). Taste and season with salt and pepper. Lightly mash the beans with a fork, being careful not to scratch the pot. You may want to transfer the ingredients to a bowl to mix things together.

4. Serve slathered on the toasted baguette slices, topped with extra chopped olives.

Preparation tip: If you cook the beans and let them marinate in their seasonings for a day or two before mashing (in an airtight container in the refrigerator), the crostini will have even more flavor.

PER SERVING Calories: 94; Total fat: 2g; Protein: 5g; Sodium: 178mg; Fiber: 3g

Caponata

Serve this hearty spread with a big loaf of crusty bread, inviting your guests to rip off large chunks and dip or spoon the hearty vegetable goodness on top. Caponata also works nicely as a sauce for pasta or couscous, topped with toasted pine nuts.
Serves 4 to 6

BUDGET-FRIENDLY, GLUTEN-FREE, NUT-FREE, SOY-FREE
Prep time: 10 minutes · Cooking setting: High Pressure, 5 minutes · Release: Quick · Total time: 25 minutes

---

* ✭ 4 tomatoes, diced
* ✭ 1 eggplant, cubed
* ✭ 1 onion, diced
* ✭ 1 (6-ounce) can tomato paste, divided
* ✭ ½ cup pitted green olives, chopped
* 2 tablespoons red wine vinegar
* 1 to 2 tablespoons unrefined sugar or brown sugar
* ¼ to ½ teaspoon salt, plus more as needed
* Freshly ground black pepper

1. In your electric pressure cooker's cooking pot, combine the tomatoes, eggplant, onion, half of the tomato paste, the olives, vinegar, sugar, and salt. Close and lock the lid and ensure the pressure valve is sealed, then select High Pressure and set the time for 5 minutes.

2. Once the cook time is complete, quick release the pressure, being careful not to get your fingers or face near the steam release.

3. Once all the pressure has released, carefully unlock and remove the lid. Stir in the remaining tomato paste. Taste and season with more salt and pepper, if needed.

PER SERVING Calories: 154; Total fat: 5g; Protein: 5g; Sodium: 275mg; Fiber: 8g

Steamed Veggie Dumplings

This recipe takes a bit of time and effort, but the dumplings are so delicious that it's well worth it. To add more protein (if soy is not a problem for you), add some crumbled tofu or replace the carrot with tofu. Be sure to check the ingredients when shopping for dumpling wrappers, as some include eggs. Dumplings are delicious on their own, but dipping them is so much fun. ***Makes 16 dumplings***

BUDGET-FRIENDLY, NUT-FREE, SOY-FREE

Prep time: 20 minutes · Cooking setting: Sauté, 6 to 7 minutes, then High Pressure, 4 minutes

Release: Quick · Total time: 39 minutes

★ 1 cup chopped shiitake mushrooms or brown mushrooms

★ 1 cup chopped or shredded carrot

1 to 2 teaspoons toasted sesame oil

★ 1 garlic clove, minced

★ 16 vegan dumpling wrappers

1. On your electric pressure cooker, select Sauté. Add the mushrooms, carrot, and sesame oil. Cook for 6 to 7 minutes, stirring occasionally, until the vegetables are lightly browned. Add the garlic for the last couple of minutes.

2. Place the dumpling wrappers on a work surface next to a small bowl of water. Lay one wrapper out and scoop 1 to 2 teaspoons of filling into the middle. Dip your fingers in the water and moisten the edges of the wrapper. Fold the wrapper over into a half-moon shape, then press the edges together to seal. You can fold the edge over itself a few times to make a pleated edge, or wrap the ends around the filling to meet on the other side for a round shape.

3. If using a metal steamer, line it with parchment paper. If using a bamboo steamer, use just the base, not the lid. Place the dumplings in your steaming basket. ➤

4. Put a trivet in the pot, pour in a cup or two of water, and place the steaming basket on the trivet. Cancel Sauté.

5. Close and lock the lid and ensure the pressure valve is sealed, then select High Pressure and set the time for 4 minutes.

6. Once the cook time is complete, quick release the pressure, being careful not to get your fingers or face near the steam release.

Preparation tip: Serve with your favorite dipping sauce or stir together 2 tablespoons tamari or soy sauce, 1 tablespoon rice vinegar, and 1 teaspoon toasted sesame oil. Add pressed garlic and red pepper flakes for some extra kick, if you like.

PER DUMPLING Calories: 111; Total fat: 1g; Protein: 4g; Sodium: 481mg; Fiber: 1g

Spinach-Chickpea Crustless Quiche

In need of a great addition or centerpiece to a brunch? Look no further. This quiche doesn't have the exact texture of eggs, but it has amazing flavor and is high in protein, thanks to the chickpea flour. And don't forget—mimosas are vegan, too! *Serves 8*

BUDGET-FRIENDLY, GLUTEN-FREE, NUT-FREE, SOY-FREE

Prep time: 10 minutes · Cooking setting: Low Pressure, 5 minutes · Release: Natural · Total time: 25 minutes

1 tablespoon olive oil, plus more for preparing the baking dish

★ 1½ cups chickpea flour

★ 1 tablespoon nutritional yeast (optional)

★ 1½ teaspoons baking powder

½ teaspoon salt

Pinch freshly ground black pepper

1½ cups water

★ ½ cup finely chopped fresh spinach

★ 1 scallion, sliced

1 teaspoon dried mixed herbs (optional)

1. Coat a 7- to 8-inch round baking dish (ideally a springform pan) that fits into your electric pressure cooker's cooking pot with olive oil. Set aside.

2. In a large bowl, stir together the flour, nutritional yeast (if using), baking powder, salt, and pepper until smooth.

3. Add the water and olive oil and stir until combined.

4. Stir in the spinach, scallion, and dried herbs (if using). Scoop the batter into the prepared dish.

5. Put a trivet in the pot, pour in a cup or two of water, and set the baking dish on the trivet. If it's a tight fit, use a foil sling or silicone helper handles to lower the dish onto the trivet (see page 5). Close and lock the lid, ensure the pressure valve is sealed, then select Low Pressure, and set the time for 5 minutes. ➤

6. Once the cook time is complete, let the pressure release naturally, about 10 minutes.

7. Once all the pressure has released, carefully unlock and remove the lid. Let the dish cool for a few minutes before carefully lifting it out of the pot with oven mitts. Let cool for about 10 minutes more before cutting and serving.

Serving tip: This quiche is best served warm, but you can make the batter ahead of time and refrigerate it until you're ready to cook.

PER SERVING Calories: 88; Total fat: 3g; Protein: 5g; Sodium: 219mg; Fiber: 2g

Mulled Wine

Here's a festive beverage for a winter party—and being able to "set it and forget it" means you can turn your attention to other party prep. The recipe easily scales up if you like—just watch the maximum capacity of your electric pressure cooker, and don't fill it more than two-thirds full. One caution: If you want to add additional liquor to this, stir it in *after* the pressure is fully released, as the steam of higher-percentage alcohol can ignite. *Makes 3 cups*

GLUTEN-FREE, NUT-FREE, SOY-FREE

Prep time: 5 minutes · Cooking setting: Low Pressure, 1 minute · Release: Quick · Total time: 12 minutes

---

* 1 (750-ml) bottle dry red wine
* 1 orange, sliced
* 1 cinnamon stick
* 1 star anise pod
* ¼ cup unrefined sugar or pure maple syrup

1. In your electric pressure cooker's cooking pot, combine the wine, orange slices, cinnamon stick, star anise, and sugar. Close and lock the lid and ensure the pressure valve is sealed, then select Low Pressure and set the time for 1 minute.

2. Once the cook time is complete, quick release the pressure, being careful not to get your fingers or face near the steam release.

3. Once all the pressure has released, carefully unlock and remove the lid. Ladle the wine into mugs or heat-proof glasses. Or, if you're not serving yet, select Keep Warm.

Ingredient tip: Feel free to use a lower-quality red wine for this, as you won't taste the difference of a good wine—but don't use cooking wine! Consider adding some or all of the following before pressure cooking: sliced lemon, whole or grated nutmeg, 1 teaspoon whole cloves, 1 teaspoon cardamom pods, and/or 1 (1-inch) piece fresh ginger, peeled and sliced.

PER SERVING (½ cup) Calories: 133; Total fat: 0g; Protein: 0g; Sodium: 0mg; Fiber: 1g

Blueberry Cheesecake

PAGE 113

CHAPTER 8

Piece-of-Cake Desserts

Let's be honest—dessert is not the first thing you think to make in your electric pressure cooker. However, you can make some really delicious treats in there without having to heat up the oven, which is great for summer. Just make sure to thoroughly clean your pressure cooker, including the lid, before making desserts, as you don't want any unintended leftover savory flavors carrying over.

Most people think of dessert as an indulgence, but the great thing about vegan desserts is there's a lot less to feel guilty about—with no cholesterol or cruelty. Plus, you can make desserts with a lot less sugar and oil than in traditional baking, and you can add some plant superfoods to create healthy indulgences.

Spice It Up!
Cinnamon is a classic spice in desserts, and it can actually help balance your blood sugar and reduce cravings.

Nutmeg has long been used to bring extra flavor dimension to desserts like apple crumble and pumpkin pie. You need only a small amount—about ¼ teaspoon for four servings.

Cardamom is one of my favorite ways to create a different flavor twist that people may not have tried. It goes beautifully with pears, mangos, peaches, and chocolate and partners well with cinnamon or ginger. As with nutmeg, you need only a small amount.

Maple-Sweetened Applesauce

If an apple a day keeps the doctor away, why not make it into dessert? One of the powerful phytonutrients in apples helps support healthy digestive flora balance, which makes apples a great choice for finishing your day. And making your own applesauce ensures that you get more of the antioxidants from those apples than you do when you eat store-bought versions. Instead of nutmeg, a sprinkle of cinnamon on top is also delicious. ***Makes about 3 cups***

BUDGET-FRIENDLY, GLUTEN-FREE, NUT-FREE, SOY-FREE

Prep time: 10 minutes • Cooking setting: High Pressure, 4 minutes • Release: Quick • Total time: 20 minutes

---

- ★ 2 pounds apples (6 medium), peeled if desired, cored, and quartered (see tip)

  1 cup water, plus more as needed

- ★ ¼ cup unrefined sugar or pure maple syrup, plus more as needed

- ★ ¼ cup freshly squeezed lemon juice (from 2 lemons)

  ⅛ teaspoon ground nutmeg (optional)

1. In your electric pressure cooker's cooking pot, combine the apples and water. Close and lock the lid and ensure the pressure valve is sealed, then select High Pressure and set the time for 4 minutes.

2. Once the cook time is complete, quick release the pressure, being careful not to get your fingers or face near the steam release.

3. Once all the pressure has released, carefully unlock and remove the lid. Let cool for a few minutes. Add the sugar, lemon juice, and nutmeg (if using). Purée the sauce—either with an immersion blender right in the pot or by transferring to a countertop blender. Add more water if needed, and more sugar or maple syrup if you like a sweeter sauce.

Ingredient tip: Use any type of apple in this for different flavors. Granny Smith will be a bit tart; Golden Delicious will be smooth and sweet. Gala are mild, and Pink Lady are sweet, with just a touch of tang. Peel the apples if you want a smooth sauce, or leave them unpeeled for a more rustic sauce—and extra nutrients.

PER SERVING (½ cup) Calories: 69; Total fat: 0g; Protein: 0g; Sodium: 1mg; Fiber: 2g

Poached Pears in White Wine

Sometimes there's elegance in simplicity. The flavors of cardamom and cinnamon add a special flair to these pears, though if you can't find cardamom pods, this is still a delicious treat. You can keep the pears whole, peel them and slice off the bottoms so they stand upright in the pot, or halve them, scoop out the cores, and lay them cut-side up in the pot. *Serves 4*

GLUTEN-FREE, NUT-FREE, SOY-FREE

Prep time: 5 minutes · Cooking setting: High Pressure, 3 minutes · Release: Quick · Total time: 15 minutes

2 cups water

★ 1 cup dry white wine

★ 1 cup apple juice, apple cider, other pure fruit juice

★ 2 tablespoons pure maple syrup or unrefined sugar

★ 1 (1-inch) piece fresh ginger, peeled and sliced

1 or 2 cinnamon sticks

1 teaspoon green cardamom pods (optional)

★ 4 to 6 pears

1. In your electric pressure cooker's cooking pot, combine the water, wine, apple juice, maple syrup, ginger, cinnamon, and cardamom (if using). Stir to combine.

2. Add the pears. (You can keep the pears whole, peel them, and slice off the bottom so they stand upright in the pot. Or halve them, scoop out the core, and lay them cut-side up in the pot.) Close and lock the lid and ensure the pressure valve is sealed, then select High Pressure and set the time for 3 minutes.

3. Once the cook time is complete, quick release the pressure, being careful not to get your fingers or face near the steam release.

4. Once all the pressure has released, carefully unlock and remove the lid.

Serving tip: Serve the poached pears topped with non-dairy ice cream and shaved or melted dark chocolate.

PER SERVING Calories: 157; Total fat: 0g; Protein: 1g; Sodium: 2mg; Fiber: 4g

Cherry-Vanilla Rice Pudding

Cherries are a natural source of melatonin, which helps regulate sleep, so having this dessert about an hour before bedtime can help set your body up for a great night's rest. Though a simple dessert, it's made elegant by what you sprinkle on top. Try fresh fruit or berries, a sprinkle of coconut, and maybe some shaved or melted dark chocolate. Leftovers are great for breakfast! *Serves 6*

BUDGET-FRIENDLY, GLUTEN-FREE, NUT-FREE, SOY-FREE

Prep time: 5 minutes · Cooking setting: High Pressure, 30 minutes · Release: Natural · Total time: 1 hour, 5 minutes

* 1 cup short-grain brown rice

* 1¾ cups nondairy milk, plus more as needed

  1½ cups water

* 4 tablespoons unrefined sugar or pure maple syrup (use 2 tablespoons if you use a sweetened milk), plus more as needed

* 1 teaspoon vanilla extract (use ½ teaspoon if you use vanilla milk)

  Pinch salt

* ¼ cup dried cherries *or* ½ cup fresh or frozen pitted cherries

1. In your electric pressure cooker's cooking pot, combine the rice, milk, water, sugar, vanilla, and salt. Close and lock the lid and ensure the pressure valve is sealed, then select High Pressure and set the time for 30 minutes.

2. Once the cook time is complete, let the pressure release naturally, about 20 minutes.

3. Once all the pressure has released, carefully unlock and remove the lid. Stir in the cherries and put the lid back on loosely for about 10 minutes. Serve, adding more milk or sugar, as desired.

Preparation tip: If you use white rice, set the time for 15 minutes.

PER SERVING Calories: 177; Total fat: 1g; Protein: 3g; Sodium: 27mg; Fiber: 2g

Mango-Coconut Custard

Heat and pressure transform a few ordinary ingredients into a magical, creamy pudding. Warning: This can become habit-forming, particularly when you see how easy it is to make! *Serves 4*

BUDGET-FRIENDLY, GLUTEN-FREE, NUT-FREE, SOY-FREE

Prep time: 5 minutes · Cooking setting: High Pressure, 10 minutes · Release: Natural · Total time: 25 minutes

---

* 2 cups chopped fresh or frozen mango

* ½ (13.5-ounce) can full-fat coconut milk (about ¾ cup)

* 2 tablespoons cornstarch or arrowroot powder

* Unrefined sugar, for sprinkling (optional)

1. In a blender or food processor, purée the mango, coconut milk, and cornstarch. Pour the mixture into 4 heat-proof ramekins. Sprinkle a bit of sugar on top of each, if you like.

2. Put a trivet in the bottom of your electric pressure cooker's cooking pot and pour in a cup or two of water. Lower the ramekins onto the trivet, stacking them if needed (3 on the bottom, 1 on top). Close and lock the lid and ensure the pressure valve is sealed, then select High Pressure and set the time for 10 minutes.

3. Once the cook time is complete, let the pressure release naturally, about 10 minutes.

4. Once all the pressure has released, carefully unlock and remove the lid. Let cool for a few minutes before carefully lifting out the ramekins with oven mitts or tongs.

5. Let the custards cool to room temperature, or refrigerate until cooled and set.

Serving tip: To go fancy, serve these topped with non-dairy whipped cream, shaved dark chocolate, and/or fresh raspberries.

PER SERVING Calories: 246; Total fat: 18g; Protein: 2g; Sodium: 13mg; Fiber: 2g

Peach-Mango Crumble

This tropical twist on fruit crumble adds mango and coconut to classic peaches and oats. Top each serving with coconut cream or nondairy ice cream, if you like. *Serves 6*

BUDGET-FRIENDLY, GLUTEN-FREE, NUT-FREE, SOY-FREE

Prep time: 10 minutes · Cooking setting: High Pressure, 6 minutes · Release: Quick · Total time: 21 minutes

* 3 cups chopped fresh or frozen peaches
* 3 cups chopped fresh or frozen mangos
* 4 tablespoons unrefined sugar or pure maple syrup, divided
* 1 cup gluten-free rolled oats
* ½ cup shredded coconut, sweetened or unsweetened

2 tablespoons coconut oil or vegan margarine

1. In a 6- to 7-inch round baking dish, toss together the peaches, mangos, and 2 tablespoons of sugar.

2. In a food processor, combine the oats, coconut, coconut oil, and remaining 2 tablespoons of sugar. Pulse until combined. (If you use maple syrup, you'll need less coconut oil. Start with just the syrup and add oil if the mixture isn't sticking together.) Sprinkle the oat mixture over the fruit mixture. Cover the dish with aluminum foil.

3. Put a trivet in the bottom of your electric pressure cooker's cooking pot and pour in a cup or two of water. Using a foil sling or silicone helper handles, lower the pan onto the trivet (see page 5). Close and lock the lid and ensure the pressure valve is sealed, then select High Pressure and set the time for 6 minutes.

4. Once the cook time is complete, quick release the pressure, being careful not to get your fingers or face near the steam release.

5. Once all the pressure has released, carefully unlock and remove the lid. Let cool for a few minutes before carefully lifting out the dish with oven mitts or tongs.

6. Scoop out portions to serve.

Variation tip: Bags of mixed frozen fruit are perfect for this recipe.

PER SERVING Calories: 321; Total fat: 18g; Protein: 4g; Sodium: 2mg; Fiber: 7g

Strawberry-Rhubarb Crumble-Top Pie

This dish is like a crumble, but with a bottom layer to soak up all the delicious fruit juices. Strawberry and rhubarb are a classic combination, and luckily for us we don't have to wait until rhubarb season, because we can now buy it frozen to use year-round. *Serves 6*

GLUTEN-FREE, SOY-FREE

Prep time: 10 minutes · Cooking setting: High Pressure, 6 minutes · Release: Quick · Total time: 25 minutes

3 tablespoons coconut oil or vegan margarine, plus more for preparing the pan

★ 1½ cups gluten-free rolled oats

★ 1 cup walnuts

★ 4 tablespoons unrefined sugar or pure maple syrup, divided

★ 2 cups fresh strawberries, chopped

★ 1 cup chopped rhubarb

1. Grease a 6- to 7-inch springform pan or pie dish with coconut oil.

2. In a food processor, combine the oats, walnuts, coconut oil, and 2 tablespoons of sugar. Pulse until combined. (If you use maple syrup, you'll need less coconut oil. Start with just the syrup and add oil if the mixture isn't sticking together.) Press two-thirds of the mixture into the bottom of the prepared pan.

3. In a medium bowl, toss together the strawberries, rhubarb, and remaining 2 tablespoons of sugar. Scoop the fruit mixture onto the crust. Sprinkle the remaining one-third of the crust mixture over the fruit. Cover the pan with aluminum foil.

4. Put a trivet in the bottom of your electric pressure cooker's cooking pot and pour in a cup or two of water. Using a foil sling or silicone helper handles, lower the pan onto the trivet (see page 5). Close and lock the lid and ensure the pressure valve is sealed, then select High Pressure and set the time for 6 minutes. ➤

5. Once the cook time is complete, quick release the pressure, being careful not to get your fingers or face near the steam release.

6. Once all the pressure has released, carefully unlock and remove the lid. Let cool for a few minutes before carefully lifting out the pan with oven mitts or tongs.

7. Let cool for at least 10 minutes before slicing and serving. If you used a springform pan, remove the rim for easier slicing.

Ingredient tip: Swap the strawberries for apples if you want. Just aim for twice the volume of the rhubarb to keep the sweet-tang ratio the same.

PER SERVING Calories: 424; Total fat: 33g; Protein: 9g; Sodium: 3mg; Fiber: 6g

Pumpkin Pie Cups

This easy recipe offers all the flavor of pumpkin pie with no fuss—served in individual cups so no one has to fight over how big a slice they get. Although, if you want, you could make a crust and put this filling in a regular pie dish. Serve with coconut cream or nondairy ice cream, if desired. *Serves 4*

BUDGET-FRIENDLY, NUT-FREE, SOY-FREE

Prep time: 5 minutes · Cooking setting: High Pressure, 6 minutes · Release: Quick · Total time: 20 minutes

---

★ 1 cup canned pumpkin purée

★ 1 cup nondairy milk

★ 6 tablespoons unrefined sugar or pure maple syrup (less if using sweetened milk), plus more for sprinkling

★ ¼ cup spelt flour or all-purpose flour

½ teaspoon pumpkin pie spice

Pinch salt

1. In a medium bowl, stir together the pumpkin, milk, sugar, flour, pumpkin pie spice, and salt. Pour the mixture into 4 heat-proof ramekins. Sprinkle a bit more sugar on the top of each, if you like.

2. Put a trivet in the bottom of your electric pressure cooker's cooking pot and pour in a cup or two of water. Place the ramekins onto the trivet, stacking them if needed (3 on the bottom, 1 on top). Close and lock the lid and ensure the pressure valve is sealed, then select High Pressure and set the time for 6 minutes.

3. Once the cook time is complete, quick release the pressure, being careful not to get your fingers or face near the steam release.

4. Once all the pressure has released, carefully unlock and remove the lid. Let cool for a few minutes before carefully lifting out the ramekins with oven mitts or tongs.

5. Let cool for at least 10 minutes before serving.

Ingredient tip: If you don't have pumpkin pie spice on hand, substitute a mixture of ¼ teaspoon ground cinnamon, ⅛ teaspoon ground nutmeg, ⅛ teaspoon ground ginger, and 1 pinch ground allspice.

PER SERVING Calories: 129; Total fat: 1g; Protein: 3g; Sodium: 39mg; Fiber: 3g

Lemon Custard Pie

This recipe is a vegan spin on my nana's lemon tarts. *Serves 6*

GLUTEN-FREE, NUT-FREE, SOY-FREE

Prep time: 10 minutes • Cooking setting: High Pressure, 15 minutes • Release: Quick • Total time: 30 minutes

½ cup coconut oil or vegan margarine, melted, plus more for preparing the pan

★ ¾ cup coconut flour

★ ½ cup plus 2 tablespoons unrefined sugar, divided

★ 1 (13.5-ounce) can full-fat coconut milk

★ ½ cup freshly squeezed lemon juice (from 4 lemons)

★ ¼ cup cornstarch or arrowroot powder

1. Grease a 6-inch springform pan or pie dish with coconut oil.

2. In a small bowl, stir together the coconut flour, coconut oil, and 2 tablespoons of sugar. Press the crust into the prepared pan.

3. In a medium bowl, whisk the coconut milk, lemon juice, cornstarch, and remaining ½ cup of sugar until the starch is dissolved. Pour this mixture over the crust. Cover the pan with aluminum foil.

4. Put a trivet in the bottom of the pressure cooker and pour in a cup or two of water. Using a foil sling or silicone helper handles, lower the pan onto the trivet (see page 5). Close and lock the lid and ensure the pressure valve is sealed, then select High Pressure and set the time for 15 minutes.

5. Once the cook time is complete, quick release the pressure, being careful not to get your fingers or face near the steam release.

6. Once all the pressure has released, carefully unlock and remove the lid. Let cool for a few minutes before carefully lifting out the pan with oven mitts or tongs.

7. Let the pie cool to room temperature, or refrigerate until cooled and set.

Substitution tip: Swap coconut flour for almond meal if you prefer.

PER SERVING Calories: 487; Total fat: 35g; Protein: 6g; Sodium: 64mg; Fiber: 11g

Blueberry Cheesecake

In this dish, the blueberries are blended into the cake itself to act as a sweetener along with the dates, but the cake also looks lovely with extra blueberries sprinkled on top or even swirled into the filling mixture before cooking. If you don't have a high-powered blender, you may want to soak the cashews in boiling water for a few minutes before puréeing to get the smoothest texture. *Serves 6*

GLUTEN-FREE, SOY-FREE

Prep time: 10 minutes · Cooking setting: High Pressure, 6 minutes · Release: Natural · Total time: 30 minutes

Coconut oil or vegan margarine, for preparing the pan

★ 1¼ cups soft pitted Medjool dates, divided

★ 1 cup gluten-free rolled oats

★ 2 cups cashews

★ 1 cup fresh blueberries

★ 3 tablespoons freshly squeezed lemon juice or lime juice

¾ cups water

Pinch salt

1. Grease a 6-inch springform pan or pie dish with coconut oil.

2. In a food processor, combine 1 cup of dates and the oats. Pulse until they form a sticky mixture. Press this into the prepared pan.

3. In a high-speed blender, combine the remaining ¼ cup of dates, the cashews, blueberries, lemon juice, water, and a pinch of salt. Blend on high speed for about 1 minute, until smooth and creamy, stopping a couple of times to scrape down the sides. Pour this mixture over the crust. Cover the pan with aluminum foil.

4. Put a trivet in the bottom of the pressure cooker and pour in another cup or two of water. Using a foil sling or silicone helper handles, lower the pan onto the trivet (see page 5). Close and lock the lid and ensure the pressure valve is sealed, then select High Pressure and set the time for 6 minutes. ➤

5. Once the cook time is complete, let the pressure release naturally, about 10 minutes.

6. Once all the pressure has released, carefully unlock and remove the lid. Let cool for a few minutes before carefully lifting out the pan with oven mitts.

7. Let the cake cool to room temperature, or refrigerate until cooled and set.

Ingredient tip: The crust works best if you use soft Medjool dates. If you can find only pitted dates from the baking section of the grocery store, soak them in boiling water for 10 minutes, then drain them before you purée. You will also need to process these harder dates for a few minutes before they break up enough to make a sticky texture with the oats.

PER SERVING Calories: 405; Total fat: 21g; Protein: 10g; Sodium: 147mg; Fiber: 6g

Fudgy Brownies

Making brownies with a base of melted chocolate ensures that they'll be rich and fudgy. You can use store-bought applesauce, or you can make your own Maple-Sweetened Applesauce (page 104). Bittersweet baking chocolate works perfectly for this recipe. *Makes 3*

BUDGET-FRIENDLY, NUT-FREE, SOY-FREE

Prep time: 10 minutes · Cooking setting: High Pressure, 5 minutes · Release: Quick · Total time: 20 minutes

---

★ 3 ounces dairy-free dark chocolate

1 tablespoon coconut oil or vegan margarine

★ ½ cup applesauce

★ 2 tablespoons unrefined sugar

★ ⅓ cup all-purpose flour

½ teaspoon baking powder

Pinch salt

1. Put a trivet in your electric pressure cooker's cooking pot and pour in a cup or two of two of water. Select Sauté or Simmer.

2. In a large heat-proof glass or ceramic bowl, combine the chocolate and coconut oil. Place the bowl over the top of your pressure cooker, as you would a double boiler. Stir occasionally until the chocolate is melted, then turn off the pressure cooker.

3. Stir the applesauce and sugar into the chocolate mixture. Add the flour, baking powder, and salt and stir just until combined. Pour the batter into 3 heat-proof ramekins. Put them in a heat-proof dish and cover with aluminum foil. Using a foil sling or silicone helper handles, lower the dish onto the trivet (see page 5). (Alternately, cover each ramekin with foil and place them directly on the trivet, without the dish.) Close and lock the lid and ensure the pressure valve is sealed, then select High Pressure and set the time for 5 minutes. ➤

4. Once the cook time is complete, quick release the pressure, being careful not to get your fingers or face near the steam release.

5. Once all the pressure has released, carefully unlock and remove the lid. Let cool for a few minutes before carefully lifting out the dish, or ramekins, with oven mitts or tongs. Let cool for a few minutes more before serving.

Serving tip: Top with fresh raspberries and an extra drizzle of melted chocolate.

PER SERVING Calories: 316; Total fat: 14g; Protein: 5g; Sodium: 68mg; Fiber: 5g

Pressure Cooking Time Charts

The following charts provide approximate times for a variety of foods. To begin, you may want to cook for a minute or two less than the times listed; you can always simmer foods at natural pressure to finish cooking.

Keep in mind that these times are for foods partially submerged in water (or broth) or steamed, and for foods cooked alone. Depending on the recipe, the same foods may have different cooking times because of the use of additional ingredients, the presence of cooking liquids, or the direction for a different release method than the one listed in the following charts.

For any foods labeled with "Natural" release, allow at least 15 minutes of natural pressure release before quick-releasing any remaining pressure.

Beans and Legumes

When cooking beans, if you have a pound or more, it's best to use low pressure and increase the cooking time by a minute or two (with larger amounts, there's more chance for foaming at high pressure). If you have less than a pound, high pressure is fine. A little oil in the cooking liquid will reduce foaming.

Unless a shorter release time is indicated, let the beans release naturally for at least 15 minutes, then quick-release any remaining pressure.

	Minutes under Pressure (Unsoaked)	Minutes under Pressure (Soaked in salted water)	Pressure	Release
Black beans	22	10	High	Natural
	25	12	Low	
Black-eyed peas	12	5	High	Natural for 8 minutes, then quick
	15	7	Low	
Cannellini beans	25	8	High	Natural
	28	10	Low	
Chickpeas (garbanzo beans)	18	3	High	Natural for 3 minutes, then quick
	20	4	Low	
Kidney beans	25	8	High	Natural
	28	10	Low	
Lentils	10	not recommended	High	Quick
Lima beans	15	4	High	Natural for 5 minutes, then quick
	18	5	Low	
Navy beans	18	8	High	Natural
	20	10	Low	
Pinto beans	25	10	High	Natural
	28	12	Low	
Soybeans, fresh (edamame)	1	not recommended	High	Quick
Soybeans, dried	25	12	High	Natural
	28	14	Low	
Split peas (unsoaked)	5 (firm peas) to 8 (soft peas)	not recommended	High	Natural

Grains

To prevent foaming, it's best to rinse these grains thoroughly before cooking or include a small amount of butter or oil with the cooking liquid.

	Liquid per 1 Cup of Grains	Minutes under Pressure	Pressure	Release
Arborio (or other medium-grain) rice	1½ cups	6	High	Quick
Barley, pearled	2½ cups	10	High	Natural
Brown rice, medium-grain	1½ cups	6–8	High	Natural
Brown rice, long-grain	1½ cups	13	High	Natural for 10 minutes, then quick
Buckwheat	1¾ cups	2–4	High	Natural
Farro, pearled	2 cups	6–8	High	Natural
Farro, whole-grain	3 cups	22–24	High	Natural
Oats, rolled	3 cups	3–4	High	Quick
Oats, steel-cut	4 cups	12	High	Natural
Quinoa	2 cups	2	High	Quick
Wheat berries	2 cups	30	High	Natural for 10 minutes, then quick
White rice, long-grain	1½ cups	3	High	Quick
Wild rice	2½ cups	18–20	High	Natural

Vegetables

The cooking method for all the following vegetables is steaming; if the vegetables are cooked in liquid, the times may vary. Green vegetables will be tender-crisp; root vegetables will be soft.

	Prep	Minutes under Pressure	Pressure	Release
Acorn squash	Halved	9	High	Quick
Artichokes, large	Whole	15	High	Quick
Beets	Quartered if large; halved if small	9	High	Natural
Broccoli	Cut into florets	1	Low	Quick
Brussels sprouts	Halved	2	High	Quick
Butternut squash	Peeled, ½" chunks	8	High	Quick
Cabbage	Sliced	5	High	Quick
Carrots	½"–1" slices	2	High	Quick
Cauliflower	Cut into florets	1	Low	Quick
Cauliflower	Whole	6	High	Quick
Green beans	Cut in half or thirds	1	Low	Quick
Potatoes, large, russet (for mashing)	Quartered	8	High	Natural for 8 minutes, then quick
Potatoes, red	Whole if less than 1½" across, halved if larger	4	High	Quick
Spaghetti squash	Halved lengthwise	7	High	Quick
Sweet potatoes	Halved lengthwise	8	High	Natural

Measurement Conversion Tables

Volume Equivalents (Liquid)

U.S. Standard	U.S. Standard (ounces)	Metric (approximate)
2 tablespoons	1 fl. oz.	30 mL
¼ cup	2 fl. oz.	60 mL
½ cup	4 fl. oz.	120 mL
1 cup	8 fl. oz.	240 mL
1½ cups	12 fl. oz.	355 mL
2 cups or 1 pint	16 fl. oz.	475 mL
4 cups or 1 quart	32 fl. oz.	1 L
1 gallon	128 fl. oz.	4 L

Oven Temperatures

Fahrenheit (F)	Celsius (C) (approximate)
250°	120°
300°	150°
325°	165°
350°	180°
375°	190°
400°	200°
425°	220°
450°	230°

Volume Equivalents (Dry)

U.S. Standard	Metric (approximate)
1/8 teaspoon	0.5 mL
¼ teaspoon	1 mL
½ teaspoon	2 mL
¾ teaspoon	4 mL
1 teaspoon	5 mL
1 tablespoon	15 mL
¼ cup	59 mL
1/3 cup	79 mL
½ cup	118 mL
2/3 cup	156 mL
¾ cup	177 mL
1 cup	235 mL
2 cups or 1 pint	475 mL
3 cups	700 mL
4 cups or 1 quart	1 L

Weight Equivalents

U.S. Standard	Metric (approximate)
½ ounce	15 g
1 ounce	30 g
2 ounces	60 g
4 ounces	115 g
8 ounces	225 g
12 ounces	340 g
16 ounces or 1 pound	455 g

The Dirty Dozen and the Clean Fifteen™

A nonprofit environmental watchdog organization called Environmental Working Group (EWG) looks at data supplied by the US Department of Agriculture (USDA) and the Food and Drug Administration (FDA) about pesticide residues. Each year it compiles a list of the best and worst pesticide loads found in commercial crops. You can use these lists to decide which fruits and vegetables to buy organic to minimize your exposure to pesticides and which produce is considered safe enough to buy conventionally. This does not mean they are pesticide-free, though, so wash these fruits and vegetables thoroughly. The list is updated annually, and you can find it online at EWG.org/FoodNews.

THE DIRTY DOZEN*

> strawberries
> spinach
> kale
> nectarines
> apples
> grapes
> peaches
> cherries
> pears
> tomatoes
> celery
> potatoes

*Additionally, nearly
three-quarters of hot pepper
samples contained pesticide residues.

THE CLEAN FIFTEEN

> avocados
> sweet corn**
> pineapples
> sweet peas (frozen)
> onions
> papayas**
> eggplants
> asparagus
> kiwis
> cabbages
> cauliflower
> cantaloupes
> broccoli
> mushrooms
> honeydew melons

**A small amount of sweet corn, papaya, and
summer squash sold in the United States is
produced from genetically modified seeds.
Buy organic varieties of these crops if you
want to avoid genetically modified produce.

Grocery List

Grocery List

Recipe Notes

Recipe Notes

Resources

Barbara Schieving and Jennifer Schieving McDaniel's website:

www.pressurecookingtoday.com

Jill Nussinow, *Vegan Under Pressure (Boston, MA: Houghton Mifflin Harcourt, 2016).*

Jill Nussinow's website: www.theveggiequeen.com

JL Fields, *Vegan Pressure Cooking (Beverly, MA: Fair Winds Press, 2015).*

JL Fields's website: www.jlgoesvegan.com

Laura Pazzaglia's website: www.hippressurecooking.com

My interview with JL Fields: https://youtu.be/pusav7obyMI

References

Gibbons, Ann. "The Evolution of Diet." *National Geographic*. www.nationalgeographic.com/foodfeatures/evolution-of-diet/.

Larsen, Linda. "Pressure Cooker Basics." The Spruce Eats. Last modified January 15, 2019. www.thespruceeats.com/all-about-pressure-cookers-474755.

Oldways Whole Grains Council. "Storing Whole Grains." https://wholegrainscouncil.org/recipes/cooking-whole-grains/storing-whole-grains.

Index

Acknowledgments

First and foremost, thank you to Jill Nussinow and JL Fields, the vegan pressure cooking pioneers who have inspired so many people to get a pressure cooker—including me!—and taught them how to use it to make amazing vegan meals. You both inspire me so much in so many ways.

I'm so grateful to my recipe testers: Marianne, Jane, Mary, Denise, Jill, Janis, Cara, Merle, and Jenny. You ladies are the best and I had so much fun sharing this process with you!

It's such a pleasure to work with the team at Callisto, and I want to send a big thank you to my editor, Marisa, and everyone who made this book come together.

There was never a better manager and break-time enforcer than Otto, the cat-man. He always makes sure we take time for treats and is there for snuggles at the end of a long day.

My dad gave me the electric pressure cooker I used to develop and test all these recipes, plus the knife that cut all the veggies that went into them. Dad, you've always been my biggest cheerleader and I love you so much for everything you do for me.

Alex, your support means the world to me. I know I could do all of this on my own, but you make sure I stay sane and you always know just when I need a pineapple.

About the Author

Heather Nicholds is a certified holistic nutritionist dedicated to helping you get all the nutrients and energy you need from plant foods. She helps vegans (or the veg-curious) nourish their bodies through easy, wholesome, and delicious plant-based meals. She has spoken at BlogHer Food and Toronto Veg-Fest. Her work has been featured in *Shape*, One Green Planet, HuffingtonPost, and Greatist. She's also a runner, environmentalist, Canadian, figure skater, small-airplane pilot, and mango aficionado. Learn more at veganook.com.

CPSIA information can be obtained
at www.ICGtesting.com
Printed in the USA
BVHW050734130819
555690BV00001B/1